The New Covenant

Watchman Nee
& Witness Lee

Published by

Living Stream Ministry
1853 W. Ball Road, P.O. Box 2121,
Anaheim, CA 92804 U.S.A.

First Edition, 3,500 copies. October 1981.

Printed in the United States of America

TABLE OF CONTENTS

PREFACE

The new covenant is full of God's grace. All who belong to the Lord and want to enjoy this grace must know the new covenant, yet how regrettable that the new covenant is so little known or understood by so many who belong to the Lord. Therefore, we are burdened to give some messages concerning the new covenant.

The new covenant, however, is too broad a topic for our limited learning, our limited experience, and our limited words. We cannot possibly make it clear or be complete. Nevertheless, we look to God for His grace that we may minister to His children something of what we have received, learned, and experienced before the Lord. We earnestly ask God that He would let us know a little of the new covenant and lead us into spiritual reality.

The Gospel Bookroom
Taiwan
November, 1955

AUTHOR'S PREFACE

TO THE AMERICAN EDITION

The first section of the book, on the truth of the new covenant, from chapter one through chapter six, was given by Brother Watchman Nee in a conference held in Shanghai in 1931. The second section, on the experience of the new covenant, chapters seven and eight, was messages given to the church in Shanghai in 1949 by Brother Witness Lee. The two were put together and published as a book by Brother Nee's Gospel Book Room in Shanghai before he was imprisoned in 1952.

INTRODUCTION

Scripture Reading:

Matthew 26:28: "For this is My blood of the covenant, which is poured out for many for forgiveness of sins." Many ancient authorities insert "new" before "covenant."

Hebrews 8:8-13: "For finding fault with them He says, Behold, the days are coming, says the Lord, and I will consummate a new covenant with the house of Israel and with the house of Judah, not according to the covenant which I made with their fathers in the day when I took them by their hand to lead them out of the land of Egypt; because they did not continue in My covenant, and I disregarded them, says the Lord. For this is the covenant which I will covenant with the house of Israel after those days, says the Lord: I will impart My laws into their mind, and on their hearts I will inscribe them, and I will be God to them, and they shall be a people to Me. And they shall by no means teach each one his fellow citizen and each one his brother, saying, Know the Lord, for all shall know Me from the little one to the great among them. For I will be propitious to their unrighteousnesses, and their sins I will by no means remember anymore. In saying new, He has made the first old. Now that which is becoming old and growing decrepit is near to disappearing."

Hebrews 10:16: "This is the covenant which I will covenant with them after those days, says the Lord: I will put My laws upon their hearts and upon their minds I will inscribe them."

Jeremiah 31:31-34: "Behold, the days come, saith Jehovah, that I will make a new covenant with the house of Israel, and with the house of Judah: not according to the covenant that I made with their fathers in the day that I took them by the hand to bring them out of the land of Egypt; which my covenant they brake, although I was a husband unto them, saith Jehovah. But this is the covenant that I will make with the house of Israel after those days, saith Jehovah: I will put my law in their inward parts, and in their heart will I write it; and I will be their God, and they shall be my people. And they shall teach no more every man his neighbor, and every man his brother, saying, Know Jehovah; for they shall all know me, from the least of them unto the greatest of them, saith Jehovah: for I will forgive their iniquity, and their sin will I remember no more."

Second Corinthians 3:6: "Who also made us sufficient as ministers of a new covenant; not of the letter, but of the spirit: for the letter killeth, but the spirit giveth life."

Hebrews 13:20-21: "Now the God of peace Who brought up from among the dead our Lord Jesus, the great Shepherd of the sheep, by the blood of an eternal covenant, equip you in every good work for the doing of His will, doing in us that which is well-pleasing in His sight through Jesus Christ, to Whom be the glory forever and ever, Amen."

(1) The new covenant is the basis of all spiritual life. Our sins can be forgiven and our conscience can have peace because we have the new covenant. We can obey God and do what He pleases because we have the new covenant. We can also have direct fellowship with God and a deeper inward knowledge of Him because we have the new covenant. Without the new covenant we would have no confidence that our sins are forgiven. It would be difficult for us to obey God and do His will or to have anything deeper than an external and ordinary fellowship with God and knowledge of God. But, praise God, we have the new covenant! And this new covenant is a covenant which He has established. Therefore, we can rest upon this covenant.

The brother who wrote "Rock of Ages, Cleft for Me," had tuberculosis of the lung for over ten years. When he was very ill he wrote a hymn in which one of the stanzas says:

Resting in the Lord's faithfulness—how sweet it is!
    For His love is truly wonderful.
Resting in the Lord's gracious covenant—how sweet!
    For His covenant is forever dependable.*

He knew what a covenant is. Therefore, he could rest upon the Lord's covenant.

(2) God's eternal purpose is made manifest in the new covenant. Therefore, if anyone belonging to the Lord does not know what the new covenant is, he will be unable to know God's eternal purpose experientially. We know that "death reigned from Adam until Moses," and that "sin reigned in death" (Rom. 5:14, 21). In that age, God's eternal purpose was not revealed. Although God preached the gospel beforehand unto Abraham, saying, "In you all the nations shall be blessed" (Gal. 3:8), we see here just a foreshadowing of grace, not grace itself. "The law was given through Moses" (John 1:17), but the law came in, as it were, by the way (Rom. 5:20). The law does not have any part in the scheme of God's eternal purpose. "The prophets and the law prophesied until John" (Matt. 11:13), but "grace and reality came through Jesus Christ" (John 1:17). Therefore, it was not until Christ that the age of grace came and there was the new covenant, thus enabling us to see God's eternal purpose.

God's eternal purpose is revealed in the new covenant. Therefore, we need to know the new covenant, for only in so doing can we expect God's eternal purpose to be accomplished in us. Without knowing the new covenant we cannot touch the hub of salvation. At best, we can only

*(Because the exact wording of the original could not be traced, a paraphrase is given here.)

touch a little on the periphery. If we know something of the new covenant, we may say that we have touched a great treasury in the universe.

What is God's eternal purpose? Simply speaking, God's eternal purpose is to work Himself into the man whom He created. God delights to enter into man and unite Himself with man that man may have His life and His nature. Before the foundation of the world, that is, in eternity, before the beginning of time, before He created heaven and earth and before He created all things and the human race, He had such a purpose. He wanted man to have His sonship; He wanted man to be like Himself; He wanted man to be glorified (Eph. 1:4, 5; Rom. 8:30). Therefore, when He created man, He created him in His own image (Gen. 1:27).

In the beginning, in the Garden of Eden, we see the tree of life and the tree of the knowledge of good and evil. God put the man whom He had made into the Garden of Eden. He only forbade man to eat the fruit from the tree of the knowledge of good and evil. In other words, He was implying that the fruit from the tree of life should be eaten. But this required that man himself must make an active choice. According to the revelation of the Scriptures, we know that the tree of life denotes God (Psa. 36:9; John 1:4, 11:25, 14:6; 1 John 5:12). If man had eaten the fruit from the tree of life, he would have had life, and God would have entered into man. But we know that the first man whom God made, that is, the first Adam, failed and became fallen. Not only did he fail to receive God's life, but he ate the fruit from the tree of the knowledge of good and evil and became alienated from God who gave life. But how we need to thank God and praise Him, for although the first man failed and fell, the second man, that is, the last Adam (1 Cor. 15:45, 47), accomplished God's eternal purpose!

In the universe there is at least one Person who is mingled with God. He is Jesus the Nazarene who is both God and man, man and God. This is the Lord Jesus, the

"Word" who "became flesh and tabernacled among us, ...
full of grace and reality" (John 1:14). Although no one has
ever seen God, there is one Person, the only begotten Son
in the bosom of the Father, who has declared Him (John
1:18). He is both God and man, and God's intention is to
work Him into man. God desires man to be conformed to
the image of His Son (Rom. 8:28, 29), and to bring man to
the state where He intended him to be, a state where he
can please God. This is God's eternal purpose; this is the
new covenant.

(3) We say that today is the age of the new covenant.
What does this mean? Here we can only speak briefly, but
in chapter three we shall speak in more detail. We know
that God has never made any covenant with the Gentiles.
Since we, the Gentiles, do not have an old covenant, how
can we have a new one? Hebrews 8:8 tells us clearly that
one day God will make a new covenant with the house of
Israel and with the house of Judah. Strictly speaking, this
covenant will not be set up until "after those days" (Heb.
8:10), referring to the beginning of the millenium. If this is
so, how can we say that today is the age of the new
covenant? It is because the Lord is treating His church
according to the principle of the new covenant, bringing
the church under the principle of the new covenant. He
desires the church to have dealings and negotiations with
Him according to this covenant until He accomplishes
what He desires to accomplish.

The Lord said, "This is My blood of the covenant ..."
(Matt. 26:28). He established the new covenant with His
blood so that we can have a foretaste of the blessings of
the new covenant. Therefore, we say that today is the age
of the new covenant. This is due to the Lord's special
grace. Consequently, we must know what the new
covenant is in experience, for only thus are we able to say
that we are those who are living in the age of the new
covenant.

(4) To know what the new covenant is, we must first

know what a covenant is. Furthermore, to know what a covenant is we must first know what God's facts and promises are. Therefore, we must speak first about God's facts and promises. Then we shall go on to see what God's covenant and the new covenant are, and what the characteristics of the content of the new covenant are. We shall also mention specifically how the law was put into man and written upon his heart, what the power of the operation of life in us is, how God became our God in the law of life, and how we can have the inward knowledge that we may know God in a deeper way.

CHAPTER ONE

GOD'S PROMISES AND FACTS

In God's Word there are some portions which speak of the responsibilities that God requires of man and other portions which speak of the grace that God bestows on man. In other words, there are those portions which speak of God's requirements and those which speak of God's grace. For example, there are many commandments, laws, and teachings which are indications that God wants man to bear responsibility. These are God's requirements for man. On the other hand, there are the spiritual blessings in the heavenlies (Eph. 1:3), and the inheritance which is incorruptible, undefiled, and which fadeth not away, reserved in heaven for us (1 Pet. 1:4). These are the things which God delights to give to us and which He has accomplished for us; this is the grace which God has bestowed upon us.

God's Word in the aspect of grace may be summed up into three categories: (1) the promises of God to us, (2) the facts which God has accomplished for us, and (3) the covenants which God has made with man which He Himself will definitely fulfill. God's promises are different from God's facts. God's promises and God's facts are also different from God's covenants. God's covenants include God's promises and God's facts. Here is a simple chart:

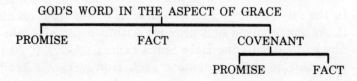

GOD'S WORD IN THE ASPECT OF GRACE

PROMISE   FACT   COVENANT

PROMISE   FACT

GOD'S PROMISES

Now let us see what is meant by God's promises. A promise is different from a fact. Promise is related to the future, while fact is related to the past. Promise is something to be done, while fact is something already done. Promise means that God will do something for man, while fact means that God has already done something for man. Promise means if you do such and such, then I will do such and such. Fact means that God loves us and, knowing our impotence, has accomplished something for us. Many of the promises are conditional. If we fulfill the conditions, we shall receive what has been promised. Facts do not require our supplication. We only need to see that the facts are facts and believe them as such.

Some examples will help to show the difference between promise and fact. For example, the Lord Jesus comforted the disciples by saying, "Let not your heart be troubled; believe in God, believe also in Me ... for I go to prepare a place for you. And if I go and prepare a place for you, I am coming again and will receive you to Myself" (John 14:1-3). This is a promise. It became a fact when the Lord came again as the Spirit.

Later, the Lord told the disciples, "It is expedient for you that I go away; for if I do not go away, the Comforter will not come to you; but if I go, I will send Him to you" (John 16:7). This is a promise. This promise became a fact on the day of the Lord's resurrection when He breathed into His disciples and said to them, "Receive the Holy Spirit" (John 20:19-22).

Again, the Lord Jesus told His disciples, "And behold, I send forth the promise of my Father upon you: but tarry ye in the city, until ye be clothed with power from on high" (Luke 24:49). This is a promise within a promise. On the day of Pentecost the Holy Spirit came (Acts 2:1-4). At that time this promise became a fact. However, this promise was conditonal; that is, the disciples had to tarry in the city.

Let us use another illustration to show the difference between promise and fact. Suppose A and B were friends. A became sick and unable to work; neither did he have money to buy the things which he needed. B loved A and told him, "Tomorrow morning I will come to do your work and bring you some money to buy the things you need." This was B's promise to A. The next morning B did come to A's house to do the work and also to give him some money to buy the things he needed. This means that B's promise to A has become a fact. If A believed B's promise, that is, if he believed B's word to be reliable, he would have hope and rest from the day the promise was given, and on the following day he would have the practical enjoyment of it.

Principles Concerning the Promises of God

God's Word shows us several principles concerning His promises. Here are some examples:

(1) "Honor your father and mother, which is the first commandment with a promise, that it may be well with you, and that you may live long on the earth" (Eph. 6:2-3). This promise is *conditional*. Not everyone will be well and live long; only those who honor their parents will be well and live long. If a person does not fulfill the condition mentioned here, he will not receive the promised blessing of well-being and long life.

(2) "Now, O Lord God, let thy promise unto David my father be established" (2 Chron. 1:9). The word "established" may also be rendered "fulfilled." This means that we need to *ask God to fulfill* His promise; that is, the promise requires prayer in order that it may be fulfilled (cf. 1 Kings 8:56).

(3) "After the number of the days in which ye spied out the land, even forty days, for every day a year, shall ye bear your iniquities, even forty years, and ye shall know

my alienation [margin, the revoking of my promise]"
(Num. 14:34). This means that if a man is unfaithful
towards God's promise and does not fulfill the conditions
accompanying it, the promise *may be revoked*. For
example, of all the children of Israel who came out of
Egypt, only Caleb and Joshua entered into Canaan. The
rest died in the wilderness (Num. 26:65). This shows that
God revoked His promise to those unfaithful ones. As for
Jacob and Joseph, although they died in Egypt, they were
buried in Canaan. Because they were faithful to God even
unto death, God did not revoke His promise (Gen. 46:3-4;
49:29-32; 50:12-13, 24-25; Josh. 24:32).

(4) "For not through the law was the promise to
Abraham or to his seed that he should be the heir of the
world, but through the righteousness of faith. For if the
heirs are of the law, faith has been made void, and the
promise made of none effect" (Rom. 4:13-14). This means
that if a man apart from God acts by the strength of his
flesh or adds something to the promise, it is possible that
the promise may become of none effect.

(5) "And these all, having obtained testimony through
their faith, did not obtain the promise, God having in view
something better concerning us, that apart from us they
should not be made perfect" (Heb. 11:39-40). And, "For you
have need of endurance in order that, having done the will
of God, you may receive the promise" (Heb. 10:36). This
means that we must *endure* until a certain time, and then
we will obtain what God has promised.

From these Scriptures we see the following four
principles concerning God's promises: (1) God's promise
requires our prayer that it may be fulfilled; (2) If God's
promise is conditional, man must fulfill His condition in
order to obtain the promise; otherwise, the promise may be
revoked; (3) If, apart from God's promise, man uses the
strength of his flesh to act or to add something, the
promise may become of none effect; (4) God's promises are
fulfilled in God's time.

How God's Promise is Accomplished in Us

How can God's promise be accomplished in us? Every time we see a promise in God's Word we must really pray. We must pray until the Spirit of God is so stirred in us that we feel deeply that this promise is intended of God for us. If there is no condition attached to this promise, we can immediately exercise our faith to receive it, believing that God will act according to His promise and accomplish in us what He has promised. We can immediately praise and thank God. If the promise has certain conditions, we need to fulfill the conditions. Then we come to God through prayer and ask Him to act according to His faithfulness and righteousness and fulfill His promise in us. When we have prayed to the extent that faith rises up in us, we need pray no longer. We can begin to praise and thank God. Then, before long, we shall see that God's promise is really being fulfilled in us.

Here are a few examples:

(1) In a certain place there were several sisters who at the beginning of each year were in the habit of asking God to give them a promise to sustain them for the year. One of the sisters felt that she was weak and told the Lord of her situation. The Lord gave her this word, "Christ ... to youward is not weak, but is powerful in you" (2 Cor. 13:3). When she received such a word, she became strong. Another sister was prone to worry; whenever she considered the past or the future, she was fearful. She too told the Lord about her situation, and the Lord gave her this promise, saying, "Fear thou not, for I am with thee; be not dismayed, for I am thy God; I will strengthen thee; yea, I will help thee; yea, I will uphold thee with the right hand of my righteousness" (Isa. 41:10). The five occurrences of "I" and the three occurrences of "will" in this verse of the Word of God caused her on one hand to bow down and worship, and on the other hand to be so joyful that she praised the Lord even with tears. Later, when she

encountered difficulties and trials, she read this word back to God and even read it to herself. God's Word really established her, helped her, and upheld her through many years.

Among these sisters were many similar stories. The promises which God gave to each of them were exactly suited to their need. They sincerely asked for God's promise and obtained it. At the end of the year, when they recounted the Lord's grace, they could testify that within the year God's promise had truly comforted and sustained them many times.

(2) Another child of God, due to the needs of her living, asked the Lord to give her a promise. One day she read this word: "Let your way of life be without love of money, being satisfied with your circumstances; for He has said, I will by no means cease to uphold you, neither by any means will I forsake you" (Heb. 13:5). These words surprised her and at the same time made her glad. This promise is conditional: we must be without covetousness, and we must be content with such things as we have; then we will not be deserted or forsaken by the Lord. She said, "Amen and amen!" to this promise. In the past twenty years since that time, on the one hand she has maintained the principle of not eating without working (2 Thes. 3:10); on the other hand the Lord has truly caused the handful of flour in her barrel and the little oil in her container not to be exhausted or lacking. The Lord has not deserted her nor forsaken her.

(3) There is the case of another sister who had been sick for many years. While she was very much in despair she recalled Romans 8:13: "For if you live according to flesh, you are about to die; but if by the Spirit you put to death the practices of the body, you will live." This gave her a new turn. She dealt with what needed to be dealt with according to the Lord's light. However, she still remained ill in body. Then one day she prayed, "Lord, if Romans 8:13 is the word You have given me, I ask You to grant me

another promise." Then she confessed her weakness and her unbelief. At this time, deep within her, there seemed to be such words: "God is not a man; He will not lie." She did not know whether such words were found in the Scriptures. Then, looking into a concordance, she discovered that in Numbers 23:19 there were truly such words: "God is not a man, that he should lie; neither the son of man, that he should repent: hath he said, and shall he not do it? Or hath he spoken, and shall he not make it good?" With this her heart was filled with joy and her mouth with praises. Consequently, God also caused her illness to depart.

(4) There were some children of God who at a certain stage of their spiritual life were brought into the experience of Psalm 66. On the one hand it seemed as though, "Thou broughtest us into the net; thou layedst a sore burden upon our loins. Thou didst cause men to ride over our heads" (vv. 11-12a). But on the other hand God also gave them the promise: "We went through fire and through water; but thou broughtest us out into a wealthy place" (v. 12b). This comforted and established them.

(5) There have been several children of God who have been encompassed by trials. Every time they prayed there was the following promise which comforted and established them: "There hath no temptation taken you but such as man can bear: but God is faithful, who will not suffer you to be tempted above that ye are able; but will with the temptation make also the way of escape, that you may be able to endure it" (1 Cor. 10:13).

(6) A certain servant of the Lord was in a very heavy trial; it seemed that a great mountain loomed before him. He had climbed this mountain to the point of exhaustion; he had climbed to the extent of despair; he had climbed to the place where it seemed that there was very little left in him to look to God. The words, "unto this present hour" and "until now" (1 Cor. 4:11, 13) brought him over this high mountain. "Unto this present hour" he was still being considered the filth of the world, the very refuse of all

things; but he was still able to stand "until now." Time tests man, but God's promises enable man to pass through the test of time and remain standing "unto this present hour" and "until now."

(7) There have been some children of God who, when being tossed by the waves, cried unto the Lord. The Lord's word to them was, "Have courage; it is I; do not fear" (Matt. 14:24, 27). At this promise their troubled heart was immediately calmed. The waves could never bring them to the bottom of the sea.

Therefore, concerning God's promises we need to praise Him that they cannot be done away; every word will be established. Faith never asks for evidence, for whatever God says, He will do. Though heaven and earth may be consumed and the mountains and hills fall, he who believes in the Lord shall see His words fulfilled.

GOD'S FACTS

Concerning God's facts, although we cannot find the word facts in the Scriptures, yet in God's work we find many accomplished facts. In other words, facts are God's accomplished work.

Facts Are the Accomplished Works

In the Old Testament God promised that the Lord Jesus would be born of a virgin (Isa. 7:14). Then, "when the fullness of the time came, God sent forth His Son, come of a woman, come under law, that He might redeem those under law, that we might receive the sonship" (Gal. 4:4-5). Thus, the promise in Isaiah that "a virgin shall conceive and bear a son" has come true, has become a fact. The crucifixion of the Lord Jesus is also a fact. He offered Himself once for all and accomplished eternal redemption (Heb. 9:12). Since this is a fact, no one need ask the Lord to die again for us and redeem us from our sins.

The coming of the Holy Spirit is also a fact forever accomplished. Since this is so, no one need ask again for

the Holy Spirit to come. (This refers to the *fact* of the
coming of the Holy Spirit, not to the individual *experience*
of the coming of the Holy Spirit.)

Moreover, God has accomplished many other things
through Christ. The Scriptures reveal that all things
pertaining to life and godliness have been accomplished in
Christ. For example, Ephesians 1:3 says, "Who hath
blessed us with every spiritual blessing in the heavenly
places in Christ." Verse 4 continues with the words, "Even
as ...," and this sentence lasts until verse 14, according to
the original text. Hence, we see that all the things
mentioned in these verses are all the spiritual blessings
referred to in verse 3. This also explains 2 Peter 1:3:
"Seeing that his divine power hath granted unto us all
things that pertain unto life and godliness." All these are
in Christ. They are facts which have already been
accomplished.

With regard to God's promises, if we do not ask
concerning them, or if we do not fulfill the conditions, we
may not obtain them; the promises may become void as far
as we are concerned. But concerning God's facts, even
though we do not ask, He will still fulfill them in us. They
are facts; therefore, we do not need to ask concerning them.
(This refers to God's facts themselves, not to our individual
experiences.)

God has never asked us to do anything in order to
obtain His facts. All He requires is that we simply believe.
There may be a delay with God's promise, but God's facts
can never be late. We can never say that we have received
God's facts and then say that we need to wait a few years
for God to give them to us. What God has accomplished
and what He has already given to us in Christ can never
be postponed to some future time. If God delays His giving
to us, it is a contradiction to fact.

Consider two examples. In Ephesians 2:4-6 we read:
"But God, being rich in mercy because of His great love
with which He loved us, even when we were dead in

offenses, made us alive together with Christ ... and raised us up together and seated us together in the heavenlies in Christ Jesus." There are three "withs" and two "mades" in this verse. Are the things mentioned here God's promises or God's facts? God's Word tells us that these are all facts. It is God who has made us alive together with Christ, and it is God who has raised us up with Christ and seated us in the heavenly places with Christ. These are all accomplished facts. Since this is so, we ought to praise and thank God. We ought to take an attitude towards Satan that we have been raised up together and that we have ascended together with Christ. We should not take an attitude of hope that we may be raised up or that we may ascend. Our attitude should be one which indicates that we *have* been raised up, that we *have* ascended. We must know that there is not one of the Lord's people who has not received a life of resurrection and ascension. If we consider that this life can only be obtained by our asking for it, we do not know what God has accomplished. God has given us in Christ all that pertains to life and godliness. We do not need to ask; we only need to claim. Hallelujah, this glorious fact, this accomplished fact, this fact which Christ has accomplished, has been given to us by God in Christ!

The second example is found in Romans 6:6 which says, "Knowing this, that our old man has been crucified with Him that the body of sin might be made of none effect, that we should no longer serve sin as slaves." This verse shows us three things: (1) sin, (2) the old man, and (3) the body of sin. Sin is that very nature of sin which rules in us (Rom. 6:14; 7:17). The old man is our self which likes to listen to sin. The body of sin is our body which is the puppet of sin. Our body is that which actually commits sins. Sin rules in us and by the old man controls our body to make it commit sins. The old man represents all that is of Adam and inclines toward sin. It is this old man which listens to sin and directs the body to commit sin. Perhaps some will think that in order for man not to sin, the root of sin must be plucked out. Others may think that for man not to sin, he must painstakingly suppress his body. These are men's thoughts; what God has done is completely different. God did not deal with the root of sin; neither did He deal with our body. What He dealt with was our old man. "Our old man has been crucified with Him" (Rom. 6:6). Just as our Lord Jesus was crucified on the cross, in like manner our old man *has been* crucified with Him. This is a fact. It is a fact which God has accomplished in Christ.

The phrase, "that the body of sin might be made of none effect" may also be rendered, "that the body of sin may become unemployed." Because our old man has been crucified with Christ, the body of sin has become unemployed. Although the nature of sin is still present and active and still comes to tempt us, the old man who has been utilized by sin has been crucified with Christ. Therefore, sin can no longer be our master; we have been freed from sin. However, someone may look at himself and think that because he is still weak and still sins, he needs to ask God again to give him grace, and to work again to root out sin, that he may be delivered from sin. Someone else may think that Christ has been crucified, but that *his* old man has not been crucified. He may therefore ask God to crucify his old man. The result is that the more he asks God to crucify his old man, the more his old man seems to be active, exercising dominion over him. What is the reason for this? It is because some are only acquainted with God's promise but do not know God's fact. Perhaps they take God's fact as God's promise, treating God's fact in the same way they treat His promises. God says that their old man has been crucified with Christ, but they think that God's promise is that He *will* crucify their old man. Therefore, they continue to ask God to crucify their old man. Whenever they commit sin, they feel that their old man has not been crucified, and they ask God once again to crucify their old man. Whenever they fall into temptation, they think that their old man has not been completely dealt with by God. For this reason they feel they need to ask God to deal with their old man. They do not know the fact that their old man has been crucified with Christ, that this is an accomplished fact and is different from a promise. Therefore, they continue to beg. The result is that they make no progress, only continuing to cry out, "O wretched man that I am!" (Rom. 7:24).

We must realize that Romans 6:6 is a basic experience for every one who belongs to the Lord. We must ask the Spirit of the Lord to give us the revelation so that we may see that our old man *has been* crucified with Christ. Then, based upon the Word of God, we will be able to believe that we are dead indeed to sin (Rom. 6:11). Although at times the temptation will come and cause us to feel that our old man is not dead, still we believe what God has accomplished more than we believe our feeling and experience. Once we see that the fact is a fact, the experience will spontaneously follow. However, we need to realize that it is not because we believe, that God's fact becomes real, but because God's fact *is* real, therefore, we believe.

Faith means that since God says our old man has been crucified with Christ, we also say that our old man has been crucified with Christ. It is a fact that our old man has been crucified, a fact which God has accomplished in Christ. God cannot do any more than He has already done. We cannot do any more than believe that God's Word is true. Therefore, what is needed is not for us to ask God to do something, but for us to believe what God has already done. Whenever we believe God's facts, the experience automatically follows. Fact, faith, and experience — this is the order which God has ordained. This great principle in the spiritual life must be remembered.

Some Principles Concerning God's Facts

From what we have seen in the previous examples there are the following principles: (1) We need to discover what

God's fact is. For this, revelation from the Holy Spirit is necessary. (2) Once we see what God's fact is, we need to hold on to God's Word and believe that we are just as God's Word says. We need to believe that just as God's fact says, so we are. (3) We need by faith on one hand to praise God that we are this way; on the other hand we need to act and manifest that we are such. (4) Whenever temptation or trial comes to us, we must believe that God's Word and His fact are more dependable than our feelings. We need only to fully believe God's Word; then God will be responsible to give us the experience. If we pay attention to our experience first, we shall fail and not have any experience. Our responsibility is to believe God's fact; God's responsibility is to grant us the experience. If we believe God's fact, our spiritual life will grow every day. (5) Fact requires our faith, for faith is the only way by which the fact may be realized in our experience. God's fact is in Christ; therefore, we must be in Christ in order to enjoy the fact which God has accomplished in Christ. When we are united with Christ, we shall experience the fact which God has accomplished in Christ. We must remember that when we were saved, we were united with Christ and were put into Christ (1 Cor. 1:30; Gal. 3:27; Rom. 6:3). But many, though they are in Christ, do not abide in Christ. Since they do not stand by faith upon the position which God has given them in Christ, they lose the effect which God's fact has toward them. Therefore, though we are already in Christ, we also need to abide in Christ. By this means, God's fact will become our experience and will continue to be manifested through us.

The Need of Seeing

We have mentioned repeatedly that God's fact is something which He has already accomplished and that we do not need to ask Him to do anything. However, if we have not seen God's fact as fact, we need to ask God to give us revelation, to give us light, that we may see. It is the spirit of wisdom and revelation that will cause us to know (Eph. 1:17-18). We can ask for such a spirit. What we ask for is the vision. We do not ask that God will do that very thing again, but that He may show us that He has already accomplished that thing. We must be clear about this difference.

Following are some further examples to clarify this matter.

(1) A sister, before she had seen the fact of being in Christ, thought that she had to exercise her own effort to work herself into Christ, yet she did not know how to do it. One day upon hearing the word, "But of him are ye in Christ Jesus" (1 Cor. 1:30), she saw in her inner being that God had already put her into Christ and that she did not need to work herself in any more.

(2) Some children of God, before seeing the fact that "our old man has been crucified with Christ," either used their own effort to crucify their old man, or asked God to do it. The result was that the more they tried to crucify their old man, the more lively the old man seemed to be. The more they asked God to crucify their old man, the more confused they became. Then one day God opened their eyes and revealed to them that He *had already* crucified their old man with Christ. At that time they realized how foolish their action and prayer had been.

(3) A certain sister was not clear that the outpouring of the Holy Spirit is already a fact. One night she closed her door and read Acts 2. While reading this portion of the Word, she asked God to give her a revelation. God opened her eyes and showed her three things in this chapter: (a) that Christ has been exalted to the right hand of God, and having received the promise of the Holy Spirit from the Father, has poured down the Holy Spirit (v. 33); (b) God has made Him both Lord and Christ (v. 36); (c) this promise of receiving the Holy Spirit is for the Israelites and for their children, and also for those who are afar off (v. 39). She saw that it is a fact that the Holy Spirit has

been poured out. Since she was one who had repented and had been baptized in the name of Jesus Christ, she was included in those who were "afar off." She realized, therefore, that she had a part in the promise, that is, that she had a part in what is mentioned in verse 38, "Ye shall receive the gift of the Holy Spirit." When she saw this, she was full of joy and could not cease to praise the Lord.

Therefore, we strongly emphasize again that concerning God's fact we do not need to ask God to do that thing again; we need only ask God to show us that He has already done that thing. We need not ask God to put us now into Christ, but we do need to ask God to show us that He has already put us into Christ. We do not need to ask God to crucify our old man, but we do need to ask God to show us that He has crucified us with Christ. Neither are we asking God to pour down the Holy Spirit from the heavens; rather, we are asking God to show us that the Holy Spirit has already been poured down. (In Acts 1:13-14 we read that the Apostles with several women, and Mary the mother of Jesus, and with His brothers, continued stedfastly in prayer with one accord. Acts 2:1 says that on the day of Pentecost the disciples were all together in one place, because at that time the Holy Spirit had not yet been poured out. But Acts 8:15-17 clearly shows that Peter and John prayed for the Samaritans who had believed in the Lord, and laid hands upon them that they might receive the Holy Spirit. They did not pray for the Holy Spirit to be poured out from heaven. The outpouring of the Holy Spirit from heaven is a fact, while the coming down of the Holy Spirit upon individuals is an experience.)

We do need to ask God to show us that His facts are facts. Whenever we have the inner revelation, we can spontaneously believe and then spontaneously have the experience. We say again that we may indeed inquire of God, but what we need to ask Him for is the enlightening of our eyes to give us revelation and light that we may really see something concerning God's facts.

CONCLUSION

We have mentioned the contrast between God's promise and God's fact. Now let us summarize the basic difference between God's fact and God's promise. In the Scriptures, promise is the word spoken by God before the thing happens, while fact is the word spoken by God after the thing has happened. We must receive God's promise with our faith, while we must not only receive God's fact with our faith, but also enjoy what God has accomplished. Therefore, when we read God's Word, one of the most important things is to differentiate which is God's promise and which is God's fact. Whenever we come to a place which speaks of God's grace, telling us how God has done something for us, we need to ask whether this is a promise or a fact. If it is a promise and has some conditions, we need to fulfill the conditions and then really pray until God gives us assurance within to know that this promise is for us. Then quite naturally we shall have faith, and we shall know that God has heard our prayer. We shall spontaneously praise God. Although God's promise has yet to be fulfilled, still, because of the fact that you have faith, it seems that that very thing is already in your hand. But if it is a fact, then you may immediately exercise faith and praise God, saying, "O God, yes, it is so!" You can believe it is really so, and then act accordingly. By doing this you will prove your faith.

There are, however, a few points of which we need to be reminded:

(1) Before we ask God for His promise, we must first deal with our impure heart. Those who are full of confusing thoughts or are too emotional will very likely consider that this is God's promise for them, or that that is God's promise for them. Yesterday there was a promise, today there is another promise. To them, obtaining God's promises is like drawing from a lottery, taking one lot after another. Nine times out of ten such promises are

undependable and might be deceiving. (This does not mean that God's promises are not dependable, but that what such people *consider* to be God's promise is something they themselves have conceived, *not something which God has given to them.*) If those who have natural inclinations or hardness of will subjectively use what they have remembered of God's Word in their mind, or if they use those words of God which suit their moods, or explain God's Word in their subjective way and treat these as God's promises, their "promises" will usually be undependable. The result is that they will become disappointed, even doubtful of God's Word. Therefore, before we ask for God's promise, we need to ask Him to enlighten our heart that we may know our heart. We need to ask God to purify our heart. We also need to ask God to grant us grace, making us willing to lay down our selves so that we may quietly look unto Him. Then if God gives us a promise, we shall be spontaneously and clearly impressed from the deepest part of our heart.

(2) After receiving God's promise we need to make use of it. Charles Spurgeon once said, "O believer, I beseech you do not treat God's promises as if they were curiosities for a museum; but use them as everyday sources of comfort. Trust the Lord whenever your time of need comes on." These are words of experience.

(3) Those who really have a promise from God usually behave and act in a peaceful and stable way, as if the promise had come true. For example, when Paul was zealous for the work at Corinth, the Lord spoke to him in a vision: "Be not afraid, but speak and hold not thy peace: for I am with thee, and no man shall set on thee to harm thee." After this, he dwelt there a year and six months (Acts 18:9-11). On another occasion when Paul was on the way to Rome and ran into danger at sea, he could stand among those who were with him in the ship and say, "Be of good cheer: for I believe God, that it shall be even so as it hath been spoken unto me." He not only believed

God's promise, but also used God's promise as a promise and a comfort to others. "And when he had said this, and had taken bread, he gave thanks to God in the presence of all; and he brake it, and began to eat." This was Paul's manner and action after he believed God's promise. Such manner gave those with him a deep impression. The result was that "they were all of good cheer, and themselves also took food" (Acts 27:23-25, 35-36). A saint has said that every promise of God is built upon four pillars: God's justice, God's holiness, God's grace, and God's truth. God's justice will not suffer Him to be faithless; God's holiness will not suffer Him to deceive; God's grace will not suffer Him to forget; and God's truth will not suffer Him to change. Another saint has said that though the promise tarry, it can never come too late. These are all words of experience from those who know God.

The Psalmist said, "Remember the word unto thy servant, wherein thou hast made me to hope" (Psa. 119:49, lit.). This is a most powerful prayer. God's promise gives us a living hope. Hallelujah!

(4) Once we have seen God's fact, our faith must continue to look at God's fact, counting the fact as fact. Whenever we have a failure, we need to *discover* the reason for the failure. We need to *condemn* both the reason for failure and the act of failing. If due to our own failure we become doubtful concerning God's fact, even denying God's fact, this proves that we have *an evil heart of unbelief* towards God's fact (Heb. 3:12). At this point we need to ask God to *remove* the evil heart of unbelief.

If we hold fast the beginning of the assurance firm to the end, we have become partners of Christ (Heb. 3:14).

CHAPTER TWO

GOD'S COVENANT

In God's word of grace, three things are included: God's promise, God's fact, and God's covenant. In the first chapter we spoke of God's promise and God's fact. Now we come to God's covenant. All those who have been taught by grace will praise God and say, "How great and precious it is for God to make a covenant with man!"

God's promise is precious. When you have illness, pain, or difficulty, God's promises become streams in a dry place. God's promise is also like a shadow of a great rock in a weary land (Isa. 32:2).

But there is something which is easier to obtain than God's promise; that is God's fact. God not only gives us the promise which He will soon fulfill; He also grants us the fact which He has already accomplished. He has truly put the treasure in earthen vessels to manifest that the excellency of the power is of God and not of ourselves (2 Cor. 4:7).

Moreover, God has not only given us His promise and the fact which He has accomplished in Christ; God has even made a covenant with us. The covenant which God has made is more glorious than either His promise or His fact. God has made a covenant with man. This means that He has condescended to be bound and limited by the covenant. The reason God is willing to lose His liberty by the covenant is that we may obtain what He intended us to obtain. The Most High God, the Creator of heaven and earth, condescended to such an extent to make a covenant with man. Oh, what an unsurpassing grace! Before such a God who is so full of grace, we can only bow and worship.

THE MEANING OF A COVENANT

What is the meaning of a covenant? A covenant speaks of faithfulness and law. In the matter of a covenant, no preference and grace can be considered. A covenant must be carried out strictly according to faithfulness, justice, and law. If we make a covenant with someone, clearly recording in writing how we will perform and do not fulfill this covenant, this means we retract our words; we become unfaithful, unrighteous, and dishonest. Our moral level is immediately lowered. Moreover, the breaking of a covenant is usually punishable by law.

We see from this that God, by making a covenant with man, has put Himself into a restricted position. Originally, God could treat man as He liked. He could deal with him in grace, or He could treat him otherwise. He could save, or He could not save. If God had not made a covenant with man, He could do whatever He liked; He was at liberty. If He preferred to do something, He could do it; if He did not like to do anything, He need not do it. But once God made a covenant with man, He must be bound by the covenant. He must perform that which was clearly written.

We know that as far as the covenant is concerned, what is involved is only faithfulness, not grace. But as far as God's willingness to be bound in making a covenant with man is concerned, the covenant is the highest expression of God's grace. God condescended and seems to stand in the same position as man. He put Himself into the covenant. After He made the covenant, He had to be limited by the covenant. Whether He likes it or not, He still must do it. He cannot act contrary to the covenant which He has made. Oh, how great a thing it is for God to make a covenant with man! How noble it is!

WHY WOULD GOD MAKE A COVENANT WITH MAN?

Why would God make a covenant with man? To understand this we must start from the first instance of

God making a covenant with man. Strictly speaking, in
the Old Testament the first instance was during the time of
Noah. Before Noah, God had not made any covenant with
man. His first covenant with man was with Noah.

Through the Covenant God Shows Man His Intention

From the covenant with Noah we see that one of the
most difficult things for God is that of causing man to
understand His intention. At Noah's time, the human race
had committed sin to the uttermost. Therefore, God
intended to destroy man by the flood. But with this
intention God not only remembered Noah's family, but
also many creatures. He wanted to preserve their lives.
Therefore, God made a covenant with Noah saying, "I will
establish my covenant with thee; and thou shalt come into
the ark, thou, and thy sons, and thy wife, and thy sons'
wives with thee. And of every living thing of all flesh, two
of every sort shalt thou bring into the ark, to keep them
alive with thee; they shall be male and female. Of the birds
after their kind, and of the cattle after their kind, of every
creeping thing of the ground after its kind, two of every
sort shall come unto thee, to keep them alive. And take
thou unto thee of all food that is eaten, and gather it to
thee; and it shall be for food for thee, and for them" (Gen.
6:18-21). God wanted to preserve their life and even
considered their food. This covenant shows how loving and
tender God's heart was toward man.

Then the flood came. All creatures of flesh and blood
upon the earth — the fowls, the cattle, the beasts, the
reptiles, and the whole human race — died. Only Noah's
family and those creatures which were brought into the
ark were preserved. Thus God fulfilled His covenant.

For one year the eight members of Noah's family were
shut within the ark. They saw and heard nothing but the
surging water. When the flood finally receded, the whole
family emerged from the ark. However, they were still full
of fear. They were not certain whether or not God would

destroy the human race again with a flood. They were not sure whether or not they would encounter the same dreadful disaster again. Although they were saved, their hearts were still fearful. We know that God's judgment of the human race by the flood was far from His desire. Genesis 6:5-6 says, "And Jehovah saw that the wickedness of man was great in the earth, and that every imagination of the thoughts of his heart was only evil continually. And it repented Jehovah that he had made man on the earth, and it grieved him at his heart." We see here what God's heart was really like. Undoubtedly, the flood made a very fearful impression upon man. God's desire was to change this impression and show man His real intention. He did not desire to destroy the human race; He wanted to comfort them. *He wanted them to know His heart's intent.* Therefore, He especially gave them evidence of His intention, and He came to make a covenant with them.

And God spake unto Noah, and to his sons with him, saying, and I, behold, I establish my covenant with you, and with your seed after you; and with every living creature that is with you, the birds, the cattle, and every beast of the earth with you; of all that go out of the ark, even every beast of the earth. And I will establish my covenant with you; neither shall all flesh be cut off any more by the waters of the flood; neither shall there any more be a flood to destroy the earth. And God said, This is the token of the covenant which I make between me and you and every living creature that is with you, for perpetual generations: I do set my bow in the cloud, and it shall be for a token of a covenant between me and the earth. And it shall come to pass, when I bring a cloud over the earth, that the bow shall be seen in the cloud, and I will remember my covenant, which is between me and you and every living creature of all flesh; and the waters shall no more become a flood to destroy all flesh. And the bow shall be in the cloud; and I will look upon it, that I may remember the everlasting covenant between God and every living creature of all flesh that is upon the earth. And God said unto Noah, This is the token of the covenant which I have established between me and all flesh that is upon the earth (Gen. 9:8-17).

In this covenant God said repeatedly that there would never be another flood. In order to assure the family of Noah that they need no longer fear, this covenant was given that they might lay hold of the words of the covenant and rest upon them.

From this we see the purpose of the covenant: God has a good intention toward man. But man could not understand or see; therefore, God gave man a covenant, so that he might have some evidence to cling to. God gave man a covenant to show him clearly what His real intention was. It seems that He was opening His heart to man so that man could see what His heart was really like. Oh, the Most High God, the Creator of heaven and earth — He even cared and considered man to such an extent! Should not even the stones be touched!

Through the Covenant
God Enlarges the Measure of Man's Faith

Now let us come to the matter of God's making a covenant with Abraham. In saving his nephew, Lot, and refusing the offer of the King of Sodom, Abraham manifested his love, his zeal, his bravery, and his cleanness (Gen. 14:14-23). Then, after these things, God came to speak to Abraham saying, "Fear not, Abram: I am thy shield and thy exceeding great reward" (Gen. 15:1). This verse shows that at this time Abraham's feeling was on one hand that of anxiety, fearing that the four kings might come again and on the other hand sorrow for Lot's departure and for his own state of childlessness. It was at this time that God came to him to strengthen and comfort him. But from Abraham's answer we see that this promise of God did not fully satisfy him. He asked, "What wilt thou give me, seeing I go childless, and he that shall be possessor of my house is Eliezer of Damascus?" (v. 2). This shows that he had not yet known or seen how gracious God's promise was. He was negative. He had his own idea and his own arrangement as well. So what did God do? God said, "This man shall not be thine heir; but he that shall come forth out of thine own bowels shall be thine heir. And he brought him forth abroad, and said, Look now toward heaven, and number the stars, if thou be able to number them: and he said unto him, So shall thy seed be" (vv. 4-5). What was it that God spoke here to Abraham? It was a promise, not a fact. What about Abraham? Now he could believe God's promise; therefore, God reckoned it to him as righteousness (v. 6). Because Abraham believed in God's promise, he became the father of faith.

After Abraham believed God's first promise, the second came: "And he said unto him, I am Jehovah that brought thee out of Ur of the Chaldees, to give thee this land to inherit it" (v. 7). Did Abraham believe this promise? No, because his measure was too narrow. He became doubtful and said, "O Lord Jehovah, whereby shall I know that I shall inherit it?" (v. 8). Because the promise was too great, Abraham could not believe it. Therefore, he asked God to give him evidence to which he could cling.

How did God deal with Abraham's unbelief? What did He do? God made a covenant with Abraham (v. 18). Therefore, the establishment of a covenant makes up that which is lacking of a promise. A covenant is the best way to deal with unbelief. A covenant enlarges the measure of man's faith. Abraham may not believe God's promise, but God could not change what He had promised. Because

Abraham could not believe, God made a covenant with him so that he could do nothing else but believe Him.

God told Abraham, "Take me a heifer three years old, and a she-goat three years old, and a ram three years old, and a turtle-dove, and a young pigeon. And he took him all these, and divided them in the midst, and laid each half over against the other: but the birds divided he not ... and it came to pass, that, when the sun went down, and it was dark, behold, a smoking furnace, and a flaming torch that passed between these pieces" (vv. 9, 10, 17). What does this mean? This means that God was making a covenant with Abraham. It means that the covenant which He made was something which went through the deepest inward parts and through the blood. The bodies of the sheep and oxen were divided, the blood was shed, and God went through the halves of the oxen and the sheep. This shows that the covenant which He made will never change nor become void.

God knew that Abraham's faith was limited. God knew that He had to enlarge the measure of his faith. Therefore He made a covenant with Abraham. God not only promised Abraham what He would do; God even made a covenant with him to show that He would do it. Thus Abraham could not but believe, for if God, after making a covenant with man, did not act according to the covenant, He would be unfaithful, unrighteous, and contrary to law. By the strengthening of such a covenant, the measure of Abraham's faith was naturally enlarged.

Through the Covenant God Gives Man a Pledge

Now let us see the history of the covenant which God made with David. Second Samuel 7:4-16 speaks of the same thing as Psalm 89:19-37. However, 2 Samuel 7 does not say clearly how God made a covenant with David. It is in Psalm 89 where we find that when the Lord sent the prophet Nathan to David, what he spoke to David was a covenant. Psalm 89 and 2 Samuel 7 speak of the same

thing, not of two different things. In both of these passages
God gave His word to David and his descendants as a
pledge. He likes for man to take hold of His word and ask
Him to fulfill it. He loves for man to do this. He gave a
covenant to man as a pledge, hoping that man would ask
Him to fulfill it.

God spoke to David in a very clear way: "If his children
forsake my law, and walk not in mine ordinances; if they
break my statutes, and keep not my commandments; then
will I visit their transgression with the rod, and their
iniquity with stripes. But my lovingkindness will I not
utterly take from him, nor suffer my faithfulness to fail.
My covenant will I not break, nor alter the thing that is
gone out of my lips. Once have I sworn by my holiness: I
will not lie unto David: His seed shall endure for ever, and
his throne as the sun before me" (Psa. 89:30-36). This tells
how God made a covenant with David. If David's
descendants forsake God's commandments, God will
chasten them with a rod and with stripes. But God cannot
forsake the covenant He made with David.

Psalm 89 was written at the time the Jews lost their
country and were taken captive to Babylon. At this time it
seemed that God had forgotten the covenant He had made
with David. When the psalmist saw the situation, how the
country was lost, he told God, "Thou hast cast off and
rejected, thou hast been wroth with thine anointed. Thou
hast abhorred the covenant of thy servant: thou hast
profaned his crown by casting it to the ground" (vv. 38-39).
Here he was reminding God of the covenant He had made
with His servant. Then he immediately inquired of God by
holding on to the covenant: "Lord, where are thy former
lovingkindnesses, which thou swarest unto David in thy
faithfulness?" (v. 49). We need to pay attention to what the
psalmist said here. He prayed by holding on to the
covenant. The Holy Spirit especially allowed such a
prayer, in which a man inquired of God, to be recorded. In
this we see how God delights that man pray by holding on

to the pledge which He has given man, namely, the covenant. This causes God to be glorified. God delights that man demand Him to fulfill what He has promised in the covenant.

THE APPLICATION OF THE COVENANT

If, having made a covenant with man, God does not fulfill it, He becomes unfaithful and unrighteous. We know that the reason God makes a covenant with man is that man may become bold enough to inquire of Him and demand Him to fulfill what He has promised in the covenant according to righteousness. God is bound by the covenant. He must act according to righteousness. So those who know what a covenant is also know how to pray; they can even pray with boldness. The following are some examples:

(1) In Psalm 143:1 we read: "Hear my prayer, O Jehovah; give ear to my supplications: in thy faithfulness answer me, and in thy righteousness." Here David did not ask God to answer him according to His mercy or His lovingkindness and grace, but according to His faithfulness and righteousness. He was not begging in a poor way; he was boldly asking God to answer him. He knew what a covenant was, and by holding on to the covenant, he knew how to ask God to answer him.

(2) When Solomon finished building the temple he said, "Blessed be Jehovah, the God of Israel, who spake with his mouth unto David my father, and hath with his hands fulfilled it ..." (2 Chron. 6:4; cf. 2 Sam. 7:12-13). Then he knelt down before the congregation of Israel, raised his hands towards the heavens and said, "O Jehovah, the God of Israel, there is no God like thee, in heaven, or on earth; who keepest covenant and lovingkindness with thy servants, that walk before thee with all their heart .... Now therefore, O Jehovah, the God of Israel, keep with thy servant David my father that which thou hast promised him, saying. ... Now therefore, O Jehovah, the God of

Israel, let thy word be verified, which thou spakest unto thy servant David" (2 Chron. 6:14, 16-17). Solomon knew the covenant which God had made with David his father. Some parts had been fulfilled, but other parts needed yet to be fulfilled. Therefore, he asked God by His covenant to fulfill what He had promised. Thus, he prayed and inquired of God by clinging to the pledge which God had given, namely, the covenant.

(3) We have seen that Psalm 89 was written after the Israelites were captured and brought into Babylon. At that time, outwardly speaking, it seemed that everything was finished. It seemed that God's promise had become void, and that God had forsaken the covenant which He had made with David. Therefore, it seems, the psalmist was reminding God: "Lord, where are thy former lovingkindnesses, which thou swarest unto David in thy faithfulness?" (v. 49). This was praying by the covenant; this was praying by cleaving to the pledge which God had given in His covenant.

HOW CAN WE KNOW GOD'S COVENANT?

How can we truly know and understand God's covenant? Psalm 25:14 tells us: "The secret (lit.) of Jehovah is with them that fear him; and he will show them his covenant." We know that unless God reveals His covenant to us, there is no way to know what the covenant is. You may hear others speak of God's covenant; you may also know a little about the matter of a covenant; but unless God reveals it, you will still have no power; you still cannot hold fast God's word. Therefore, God must show it to us in our spirit.

What kind of person can have God's revelation? Only those who fear God. The Lord gives His secret only to those who fear Him, and His covenant to those who fear Him. What does it mean to fear Him? To fear means to magnify, to exalt Him. A person who fears God is one who seeks God's will with a full heart, with the intention of completely submitting to God's way. It is to this kind of person that God will reveal His secret and reveal His covenant. Those who are lazy, careless, double-minded, proud, and complacent can never expect God to reveal His secret to them. Neither can they expect God to reveal His covenant to them. The Lord only gives His secret and reveals His covenant to those who fear Him. This is the testimony of those who fear God. Therefore, if we truly want to know God's covenant, we need to learn to fear God.

CHAPTER THREE

A GENERAL SKETCH OF THE NEW COVENANT

God made many covenants with man. The obvious ones are those He made with Noah, with Abraham, with Israel at Horeb after they left Egypt, with Israel at other times (Deut. 29:1), and with David. However, besides these covenants, there is the one God made with us through the Lord Jesus Christ, which is often referred to as the new covenant. Although there are many covenants, the most important are the one which God made with Abraham and the one called the new covenant. The others cover a smaller area and are of less importance.

THE NEW COVENANT CONTINUES
THE COVENANT OF ABRAHAM

The new covenant is a continuation and development of the covenant God made with Abraham. Galatians 3 shows us that the new covenant and the covenant made with Abraham are of the same line. Between Abraham's covenant and the new covenant there is the covenant of law made with Israel (Gal. 3:15-17). However, the law was added because of transgression; it is basically an addition (Gal. 3:19; Rom. 5:20). Only the covenant made with Abraham and the new covenant are of faith and promise (Gal. 3:7, 9, 16, 17; Heb. 8:6). For this reason, they are of the same line.

Between the covenant with Abraham and the new covenant is the covenant of law which God made with Israel. This is what is referred to in Hebrews 8:7 as the "first covenant." This is also what we call the old covenant. This old covenant does not really mean the thirty-nine books from Genesis to Malachi which we commonly call the Old Testament. Strictly speaking, the old covenant began from Exodus 19 and continued until the time of the death of the Lord Jesus. The conditions in the old covenant were bilateral. This is why there were two tables of the covenant in the ark (Exo. 31:18). If the children of Israel would keep the law, God would bless them; if they broke the law, God would punish them. This is the old covenant. Before this old covenant there was an earlier one, the covenant God made with Abraham. The new covenant continues, not the old covenant, but Abraham's covenant.

THE FIRST COVENANT HAS FAULTS

Hebrews 8:7 says, "For if that first covenant was faultless, no place would have been sought for a second." This tells us that the first covenant has faults. As far as the *nature* of the first covenant is concerned, "the law is holy" (Rom. 7:12), "the law is spiritual" (Rom. 7:14), and "the law is good" (1 Tim. 1:8). But as far as the *function* of the first covenant is concerned, "by law is knowledge of sin" (Rom. 3:20), "And the law is not of faith, but he who does them shall live by them" (Gal. 3:12). This means that the law requires man to do good, but it does not give man the life and power to do good: "For what is impossible to the law, in that it was weak through the flesh ..." (Rom. 8:3). Therefore, "by the works of law no flesh shall be justified before Him ..." (Rom. 3:20). In summary, "the law perfected nothing" (Heb. 7:19). Therefore, the first covenant has faults.

We need to see that Exodus 19 through 24 are the words of God's covenant. Three months after the children of Israel left Egypt, they came to the wilderness of Sinai. There they pitched their tents beneath the mountain, and Moses went to God. God wanted him to speak to the children of Israel: "Now therefore, if ye will obey my voice indeed, and keep my covenant, then ye shall be mine own possession from among all peoples: for all the earth is mine

.... And all the people answered together, and said, All that Jehovah hath spoken we will do" (Exo. 19:1-8). After Moses declared the whole covenant to the congregation, he "took the blood, and sprinkled it on the people, and said, Behold the blood of the covenant, which Jehovah hath made with you concerning all these words" (Exo. 24:8).

In this covenant there are words such as, "Thou shalt have no other gods besides (lit.) me. Thou shalt not make unto thee a graven image, nor any likeness of any thing ... thou shalt not bow down thyself unto them, nor serve them" (Exo. 20:3-5). Could the children of Israel do this? We know that even before Moses brought the tables of the covenant down from the mountain, they were already making the golden calf and worshipping it (Exo. 32:1-8). In other words, even before the tables of the covenant were brought down from the mountain, the children of Israel had become unfaithful to the covenant. This was the fault of the first covenant.

After this, the children of Israel continued to fail in keeping God's covenant. They provoked God in the wilderness. They tried Him by testing Him and saw His works forty years. Nevertheless, they always went astray in heart; and they had not known God's ways (Heb. 3:8-10). They saw God's "works," but they did not know God's "ways." Again, this was the fault of the first covenant.

"For finding fault with them He says, Behold, the days are coming, says the Lord, and I will consummate a new covenant with the house of Israel and with the house of Judah. Not according to the covenant which I made with their fathers in the day when I took them by their hand to lead them out of the land of Egypt; because they did not continue in My covenant, and I disregarded them, says the Lord" (Heb. 8:8-9). This means that God wanted them to continue to be faithful to the covenant, but they could not. At one time they were determined to follow the Lord, yet they could not faithfully follow Him daily. Although at one time they were revived, they could not maintain their revived condition day by day. This was the fault of the first covenant.

Paul said, "For we know that the law is spiritual; but I am fleshly, sold under sin . ... For I know that in me, that is in my flesh, nothing good dwells; for to will is present with me, but to do the good is not" (Rom. 7:14, 18). Paul's experience also tells us that the law itself is spiritual, but the law could not perform, in that it was weak through the flesh (Rom. 8:3). This, too, was the fault of the first covenant.

THE NEW COVENANT BEING THE BETTER COVENANT

The first covenant had faults. Then what about the second covenant? The second covenant is the new covenant (Heb. 8:7, 13). The new covenant is enacted upon better promises (Heb. 8:6). The new covenant is not written on tables of stone, but on tables that are hearts of flesh (2 Cor. 3:3). The new covenant imparts God's laws into man's mind and inscribes them upon man's heart (Heb. 8:10). In other words, in the new covenant, the One who demands of us is God, and the One who enables us to do the will of God is also God! The new covenant is a covenant in which God gives you life and power to do the good He intends you to do, so that He may be your God and you may be His people (Heb. 8:10; Titus 2:14). The new covenant enables man to know God more deeply and in an inward way, without being taught by his fellow citizen (Heb. 8:11). Therefore, the new covenant is the covenant of sanctification (Heb. 10:29), the better covenant (Heb. 7:22; 8:6), and an eternal covenant (Heb. 13:20). We must say, "Hallelujah! How sweet and how glorious is the new covenant! What a grace it is!"

THE NEW COVENANT INCLUDES
GOD'S PROMISES AND GOD'S FACTS

We have seen before that the word of grace which God has given us includes God's promises, God's facts, and

God's covenants. We have also seen that God's covenants include God's promises and God's facts. Now let us see God's promises and God's facts which are included in God's covenants. The Scriptures show us that God's covenant is God's promise, except that God's promise was spoken by God's mouth, and God's covenant was made by an oath (Heb. 6:17). The promise binds God, and much more, the covenant binds God. When God made a covenant with Abraham He swore by Himself (Heb. 6:13-14). "Wherefore God, willing to show more abundantly to the heirs of the promise the unchangeableness of His counsel, intervened by an oath" (Heb. 6:17). For "the Lord has sworn and will not regret it" (Heb. 7:21). Therefore, a covenant limits God and binds God more than a promise.

Hebrews 9:15-18 clearly shows us that in the new covenant there are promises and there are also facts. Verse 16 says, "For where there is a testament there must of necessity be the death of him who made it." In the original text, testament and covenant are the same word. Therefore, the word covenant has two meanings in the Scriptures: first it is a covenant, or contract, and second it is a testament, or will. Hence, we can say that the new covenant is a covenant, and we can also say that it is a will.

God's Promises

A covenant cannot be established without a promise. Every covenant must have a promise. An ordinary promise does not necessarily contain any pledge, but the covenanted promise must go through a legal process; it is protected and enforced by law. Hence, God's covenant must include God's promise. Those who are deeply taught by God's grace and who deeply know Him, consider that there is very little difference between His promise and His covenant, for they know that God is faithful even as He is righteous. They believe that if God has promised, He will fulfill His promise. It is not necessary for all His promises to pass through a legal process. To them, God's promise equals His covenant. But to those who are weak in faith, there is a great difference between God's promise and God's covenant. To them it seems that the covenant is the guarantee that God's promise will definitely be fulfilled. We cannot say that all of God's promises are His covenants, but we dare to say that all of God's covenants include His promises.

Hebrews 8:6 says, "But now He has obtained a more excellent ministry; inasmuch as He is also the Mediator of a better covenant, which has been enacted upon better promises." This verse tells us that the new covenant is a better covenant because it is enacted upon better promises.

God's Facts

In God's covenant there is not only the promise, but also the testament. Hebrews 9:15 speaks of "the promise of the eternal inheritance" and verse 16 speaks of the testament. A testament, or will, indicates that there is an estate, a bequest. The things bequeathed are the facts. For instance, a father may make a will, specifying how his possessions should be taken care of and disposed. Either they are to be passed on to his son or to someone else. Then those who receive the inheritance enjoy what he bequeathed. Therefore a testament, or a will, is not composed of empty words, but must include some facts. A testament is a covenant. Therefore, we say that the covenant includes God's facts.

A covenant differs from God's promise and God's fact, but a covenant also includes God's promise and God's fact. Without the promise and fact, the covenant becomes empty words and meaningless. We thank God that He has many promises which are related to the new covenant. There are also many facts which are related to the new covenant. We must say, "Hallelujah, the new covenant is so rich and complete!"

THE AGE OF THE NEW COVENANT

When speaking of the new covenant age we must ask three questions: (1) With whom did God originally establish the new covenant? (2) When did God make the new covenant? and (3) Why is today the age of the new covenant?

With Whom Did God Make the New Covenant?

According to the Scriptures, God never made any covenant with the Gentiles. Therefore, the new covenant cannot be a covenant which God made with the Gentiles. Nor had God ever made any covenant with the church before this time. Since there was no first covenant, or old covenant, with the church, we cannot say that God made a second covenant, or a new covenant, with the church. Then with whom did God make the new covenant? Jeremiah 31:31-32 says, "Behold, the days come, saith Jehovah, that I will make a new covenant with the house of Israel, and with the house of Judah: not according to the covenant that I made with their fathers in the day that I took them by the hand to bring them out of the land of Egypt." When the children of Israel came out of Egypt, the Lord God made a covenant with them. Later God said that He would make a new covenant with them. This word clearly shows us that God made a covenant, not with the Gentiles, but with the houses of Israel and Judah.

When Did God Make the New Covenant?

In determining the time when the new covenant was made, we must take into account the words in Jeremiah 31:31 which say, "The days come." We know that when these words were spoken the days had not yet come. Verse 33 says, "But this is the covenant that I will make with the house of Israel after those days, saith Jehovah." What are the days referred to by the phrase mentioned here, "after those days"? We believe that according to the content of this covenant they refer to the beginning of the millennium. It will be at that time that God will make a new covenant with the house of Israel.

Why is Today the Age of the New Covenant?

Since the new covenant is a covenant which God will make with the house of Israel in the future, why do we say that today is the new covenant age? When we come to this point we must realize that it is altogether too wonderful and an exceeding grace. We see that in the night the Lord Jesus was betrayed, "taking the cup and giving thanks, He gave it to them, saying, Drink of it, all of you; for this is My blood of the new (lit.) covenant ..." (Matt. 26:27-28). "New covenant!" Oh, what music to our ears! How wonderful! How marvelous!

Although the term "new covenant" was written in the book of Jeremiah, still for several hundred years it was not mentioned. It was a treasure which had been forgotten. When the Lord Jesus was on earth, He never mentioned the new covenant for more than thirty years. Day after day, year after year, He never mentioned it. Why at the time when He was eating the supper with His disciples, did He take the cup and bless it and give it to them saying, "Drink of it, all of you; for this is My blood of the new covenant"? He not only mentioned the new covenant; He also said, "This is My blood of the new covenant." Oh, holy and gracious Lord, with thankful tears we worship and praise You! What a new covenant this is, full of life and full of riches! To those who do not know, it is only letters. Lord, You alone know what this covenant is. Today You have revealed this new covenant. We can say that You have opened the heavenly, spiritual treasure store, and You have bequeathed all the treasures to those whom You love. O Lord, how wonderful and gracious You are! Once again we thank and praise You.

Because of the Lord's exceeding grace, the new covenant applies to all those who are found by grace. Although it is not until "after those days" (Heb. 8:10) that

God will make a new covenant with the houses of Israel and Judah, still the Lord paid the price of His blood, enabling those whom He has redeemed to enjoy the new covenant first. From the day He died, the new covenant was established. This is the Lord's great grace, so that we may have a foretaste of the blessing of the new covenant. It is in principle the same as when God made a covenant with Abraham. He did not make the covenant with us, but with Abraham. Yet in the same way that Abraham was justified by faith, we also can be justified by faith. Likewise, the new covenant which God promised Israel for their enjoyment in the future, because the Lord has shed His blood, can be enjoyed by us today as those who have been put under the new covenant. The Lord is building us up today by the principle of the new covenant and blessing us with the blessing of the new covenant. We know that the Lord shed His blood not only for our redemption, but also for the establishing of the new covenant. Redemption is but the procedure, the path, to reach the goal. The goal at which the Lord was aiming when He shed His blood was the establishing of the new covenant. Redemption is closely related to the establishing of the new covenant, for if the problem of sin were not solved, the blessing of the new covenant could not come upon us. We thank the Lord that His blood not only solved the problem of sin, but also established the new covenant. Therefore, this age is truly the new covenant age. Oh, the new covenant age is a blessed age! We need to praise God!

THE CONTENTS OF THE NEW COVENANT

Now we shall summarize the contents of the new covenant. In later chapters we will examine its contents in more detail.

Hebrews 8:10-12 says, "For this is the covenant which I will covenant with the house of Israel after those days, says the Lord: I will impart My laws into their mind, and on their hearts I will inscribe them, and I will be God to them, and they shall be a people to Me. And they shall by no means teach each one his fellow citizen and each one his brother, saying, Know the Lord, for all shall know Me from the little one to the great among them. For I will be propitious to their unrighteousnesses, and their sins I will by no means remember anymore." This passage clearly reveals that the new covenant includes three parts: first, God imparts His laws into man's mind and inscribes them upon man's heart. God becomes their God, and they become God's people. This means that God Himself enters into man to be one with man. Second, these laws which are within man enable man to know God without the teaching of others. This is the inward knowledge of God. Third, God. will make propitiation for man's unrighteousnesses; neither will He remember man's sins. This is forgiveness.

Hebrews 8:10-11 is actually one continuous thought. Verse 12 starts another thought. Based upon the word "For" in verse 12, we see that forgiveness is already accomplished. From God's standpoint, verses 10 and 11 are His goal; therefore, they are mentioned first. Verse 12 is God's procedure to reach His goal; therefore, it is mentioned later. According to our spiritual experience, God first makes propitiation for our unrighteousnesses and forgives our sins. Then He imparts His laws into our mind and inscribes them on our heart, so that He may be our God and we may be His people; finally He enables us to have an inward, deeper knowledge of Himself.

We may list these three parts of the new covenant as follows: 1) cleansing, 2) life and power, and 3) inner knowledge.

The new covenant truly meets our need. It need not be more, and it cannot be less. What God has done is truly complete. God has saved us, and through the Lord Jesus Christ, He has given these three great blessings to us. When we have the new covenant, we have cleansing, life, and power. We also have an inward knowledge so that we may know God in a deeper way. How complete and how glorious is the new covenant! How gracious God is toward us!

CHAPTER FOUR

THE SECURITY OF THE NEW COVENANT

In Matthew 26:28 we read, "For this is My blood of the new covenant, which is poured out for many for forgiveness of sins" (marg.). This verse reveals that the blood of Christ is the "blood of the new covenant." This blood is especially for the establishing of a covenant. The new covenant was established through the blood; therefore, the new covenant is dependable; it is secure.

THE NEED FOR THE BLOOD

We need to understand why the new covenant must be established through the blood and why a covenant is effective only when it is established with the blood. To understand this we must return to the story of Eden and the requirement of the law.

We know that when Adam was cast out of Eden, he lost the position of fellowship with God. He lost life, and he also lost his inheritance. From Adam to Moses, death reigned (Rom. 5:14). From Moses to Christ not only did death reign, but sin also reigned (Rom. 5:21). This does not mean that from Adam until Moses there was no sin. Scripture tells us that "until the law sin was in the world, but sin is not reckoned when there is no law" (Rom. 5:13). God gave Moses the covenant of the law on Mount Sinai. This covenant was conditional. If man would abide by the words of this covenant, God would bless him; if man would not abide by the words of this covenant, he would be cursed (Gal. 3:12, 10). What then did the law do for man? The law brought man the knowledge of sin (Rom. 3:20).

Besides this, man was guarded, kept in ward, under the law (Gal. 3:23). This means that man was formerly under the dominion of death, because death reigned; but now he was also under the power of sin, because sin reigned.

Therefore, before Christ came to the earth, man suffered two great losses: first, he suffered because of Adam's sin, and second, he suffered because he could not keep God's law. Because death and sin reigned, man was kept far from God and could not enjoy God's presence. He became foolish and could not know God; he lost the spiritual life and power to do God's will. In Adam, under the law, what can man boast in? He can only cry out, "Wretched man that I am! Who will deliver me from the body of this death?" (Rom. 7:24). Is there then no way to solve the problem of sin and death? There surely is! By the Lord Jesus shedding His blood, these two problems are solved.

We have seen that from Adam to Moses death reigned and that from Moses to Christ not only did death reign, but sin also reigned. Praise God, the blood of the Lord Jesus has solved these two problems for us! Due to the fact that the Lord Jesus shed His blood we have been washed from our sins, and we do not have to die.

God's original intention was to impart His own life and everything He is to us. But due to our sins and the death resulting from sin, we were alienated from God. We could no longer obtain all that is of God. We lost all that God had given, and we also lost all that God intended to give us. But the blood of the Lord Jesus cleanses us from our sins. He has also restored our relationship with God (Eph. 2:13) so that all God has given and will give to us can become ours without hindrance. Therefore, the blood of the Lord Jesus not only reconciled us to God (Col. 1:20), but also brings God Himself to us (Rom. 8:32).

The blood of Christ not only accomplished redemption; it also accomplished an eternal redemption. The blood of bulls and goats, upon which the people of the Old Testament depended, only reminded them of sin every year

(Heb. 10:3-4). But Christ, through His own blood entered once for all into the Holy of Holies, having found an eternal redemption (Heb. 9:12). The blood of Christ purifies our conscience (Heb. 9:14) so that we no longer have any "conscience of sins" (Heb. 10:2). Praise God, the blood of Christ eternally and completely solves the problem of sin!

The blood of Christ enables us to receive the forgiveness of sin (Heb. 9:22; Matt. 26:28; Eph. 1:7). Just to realize this much is a most glorious thing. Those who sense the shamefulness of sin and know how hateful sin is, all realize this. But we praise God that the blood of the Lord Jesus not only solves the problem of sin and death, but it also restores the inheritance we have lost and brings us what we did not have in the past. This blood has done a most wonderful thing: it has enabled us to obtain God. The blood of the Lord Jesus not only redeems from sin so that we will not suffer its consequences, but also completely restores what we lost in the Garden of Eden and adds new things as well. The Lord Jesus said, "This cup is the new covenant in my blood" (Luke 22:20). On one hand the Lord's blood was shed for redemption. It removes on the negative side those things which damage us. On the other hand His blood was shed for the establishing of the new covenant. It restores on the positive side the inheritance we have lost and also gives us new things. Therefore, the blood of the Lord Jesus is not only for redemption but also for restoration, restoring what we have lost and bringing that which we did not have in the past.

THE RELATIONSHIP BETWEEN
THE BLOOD AND THE COVENANT

Concerning the relationship between the blood and the covenant, we can say that the blood is the base while the covenant is the contract, the writing. The blood is the base upon which the covenant is established, while the covenant is the contract established with the blood. Without the blood, a covenant cannot be established, much less become effective. The inheritance which God has given us is recorded in the contracted covenant. This is the new covenant which God made with us through the blood of the Lord Jesus. It is by this new covenant that we receive the spiritual inheritance which God has given us.

Therefore, the new covenant is an absolutely legal matter. It was established wholly according to the procedure of God's righteousness. The new covenant is not a few mere verbal statements made by God, but a contract in writing which God has established through Christ's blood for us. It is important to realize that God's salvation before the crucifixion of the Lord Jesus was all accomplished by His grace, but that after the Lord's crucifixion it was accomplished by His righteousness. This does not mean that after the Lord's crucifixion there was no grace, but only that grace is like water, and righteousness is like the water pipe. God's grace flows to us through the pipe of righteousness. Therefore, Romans 5:21 says, "That as sin reigned in death, so also grace might reign through righteousness unto eternal life through Jesus Christ our Lord." Grace reigns through righteousness. God does not give grace to man by itself; He gives grace to man through righteousness. God loves us, and the Lord Jesus came to die for us. This is God's grace. If God did not love us and give us grace, the Lord Jesus would not have come to accomplish redemption for us. But the Lord Jesus has died for us and redemption has been accomplished. Because of this, when we believe in the Lord we are saved; this salvation is through His righteousness.

We cannot say that God does not have grace. If God did not have grace, there would be no new covenant. But if all that God has given us was based only upon grace, our faith might be shaken, for without passing through the legal process grace may be discontinued. But, praise God! He not only has grace, but He expresses His grace through a covenant. In order to give grace to us, He binds Himself in a covenant. Therefore, we may say that grace appears in the form of righteousness. Such righteousness does not annul grace, but it is the highest expression of grace.

What we receive is God's grace, but God has used the blood to make a covenant with us, so that through the covenant we may ask God to deal with us according to His righteousness. We stand upon the ground of grace, but grace comes to us through righteousness. The blood of Christ has become the foundation of righteousness, so that the covenant God has made with us will not become void. We are standing upon the foundation of the blood, the foundation of righteousness, to deal with God. Therefore, God has no choice but to fulfill in us all that is in the covenant.

One experienced in the Lord has said, "God's covenant is His therapy for the unbelieving ones. He uses His covenant to heal them." For example, some may think that in order to have forgiveness of sins they must pray until they feel peace; then they will have evidence of forgiveness. But God's Word says, "If we confess our sins, he is faithful and righteous to forgive us our sins, and to cleanse us from all unrighteousness" (1 John 1:9). One thing to which we must pay attention is whether or not we have *confessed* our sins. Of course the confession spoken of here is not a careless act without the least feeling of hatred towards sin. The confession here refers to really seeing sin as sin under the light, and condemning it for what it is. Naked before God, we confess the sin we have seen; we confess the sin which we have condemned. When we confess the sins, God will forgive and cleanse us of our sins. Therefore, once we have confessed, we should believe that God has forgiven, and our hearts should have complete peace. A brother has said, "As you have done your part, is it possible that God will not do His part?" This remark is very meaningful. The problem lies in whether or not we have confessed. If we have truly confessed our sin, we should not care for our feeling; nor should we care for what others say about us. Neither should we care for the thoughts Satan sends us; we should only believe God's Word.

Therefore, the Christian's life has no other secret than living by holding on to God's Word, believing that God is faithful and righteous, and that what He has said, He will do. If we stand fully upon the covenant which the Lord Jesus has established, God will care for us and fulfill what He has said in the covenant, for He has accepted the blood of the Lord Jesus. God binds His own will to the covenant and can only move within His covenant. If He had not established a covenant with us, He could treat us as He wished. However, since He has made a covenant with us, He can only do according to what is said in the covenant. He must fulfill His covenant; He cannot be unrighteous. We praise God that He loves us and has had mercy toward us to such an extent that He cannot treat us in any way other than righteousness. There is no grace greater than this!

We must say that without the blood of the Lord Jesus we are not entitled to anything. But through the blood of the Lord Jesus we are entitled to everything! Through the blood of the Lord Jesus we have the right to enjoy all that is in the covenant. When, by the blood of the Lord Jesus, we ask God to give His blessings to us according to the covenant, God cannot be unrighteous. He must give them to us according to the covenant. This new covenant was made by the Lord with His own blood. The Lord has paid the price of the blood. Now we can ask God to accomplish upon us all that is in the covenant according to the value of the blood which is before Him.

A brother once said, "No one really knows how much the blood includes." We may not understand the value of the blood, nor do we need to see the value of the blood. But we can ask God to treat us according to the value of the blood before Him and according to the covenant which the Lord made with His blood. We need only tell God: "I want this, for You are the God of the covenant." Our God can never be unfaithful; He will not break His covenant.

The blood of the new covenant solves the problem of our sins and removes the hindrances between God and us. It also restores the inheritance we lost and enables God to give us all spiritual blessings in the heavenlies, and all things that pertain to life and godliness (Eph. 2:12-13, 18-19; 1:3; 2 Pet. 1:3). All of the things that are clearly written in the new covenant are our rightful blessings through the blood. According to Hebrews 8:10-12, the new covenant includes three very precious parts mentioned in earlier chapters: cleansing, life and power, and the inward knowledge. More will be said about these items in chapters six through eight.

The reason we do not know how to speak to God according to what is explicitly written in the covenant is that we do not know how much blessing the blood has brought us. It is important to realize that all spiritual blessings and spiritual inheritance are given to us through the covenant established by the blood! The blood is the basis upon which we receive the new covenant.

Therefore, when we ask according to the covenant we are not asking for things which do not belong to us. Rather we are claiming the items which have always belonged to us and have been reserved in God for us (1 Pet. 1:3-4). To pray according to the covenant is not to pray without basis, but to claim what God has given us in the covenant. When we pray according to the covenant, God cannot but stand on our side. Therefore, when we come to God through the new covenant established by the blood, many times we just need to claim and not to ask. This does not mean that today we do not need to pray, but that our prayer should consist more of claiming than of asking.

A brother who knows the Lord has said that since the time of Golgotha all the asking in the Scriptures should be changed to taking. Those who know the Lord, who know the place Golgotha, and who know what the blood means will say "Amen!" Brothers and sisters, we must remember that through the blood we are asking God to give us that to which we are entitled. This is why we say repeatedly that the principle upon which God now treats us is based upon His righteousness, not only upon His grace. What is offered to us in the new covenant, then, is all that we are entitled to receive. According to His righteousness God has no choice but to give us what is clearly written in the new covenant, for we are claiming it from God according to the covenant.

Sometimes it seems God has forgotten His covenant. At these times we can remind Him. In Isaiah 43:26, God says, "Put me in remembrance." God wants man to remind Him. Sometimes we can reverently speak to God in this manner, "God, we ask You to remember Your covenant, Your promised word. We pray that You would act according to Your promise and Your covenant." When we ask like this and believe like this, we will receive that for which we ask.

A GREAT PRAYER

In Hebrews 13:20-21 we read, "Now the God of peace Who brought up from among the dead our Lord Jesus, the great Shepherd of the sheep, by the blood of an eternal covenant, equip you in every good work for the doing of His will, doing in us that which is well-pleasing in His sight through Jesus Christ, to Whom be the glory forever and ever, Amen." This is a prayer of faith. This is also a great prayer in the Scriptures. The writer of Hebrews asked God, through the blood of the eternal covenant, to cause the resurrected Jesus Christ to dwell in us, so that we may do God's will and accomplish the things well-pleasing to Him. This shows us that a prayer with faith, a great prayer, is one prayed by standing upon the eternal covenant of the Lord's blood.

We need the faith to pray by clinging to the covenant. We must tell God by the covenant, "O God, I am praying to You by Your covenant." This kind of prayer is powerful and effective. Our faith in the covenant will increase our boldness in prayer to God.

We must remember that we have the right to pray to God according to the covenant. We may ask God to act according to the covenant, but without faith the prayer will be useless. All that God has given us in the new covenant is deposited as one deposits money in the bank. If we believe, we have only to draw it out.

The new covenant was established with the blood of the Lord Jesus; therefore, the new covenant is secure and dependable. Our God restricts Himself in the covenant. God condescended to covenant with man because He wants man to believe Him and draw near to Him. God humbled Himself to make a covenant so that He can give man a bond to take hold of. Man can come to ask of Him by this bond. Therefore, we can boldly sing:

> Standing on the promises I shall not fall,
> List'ning ev'ry moment to the Spirit's call.
> Resting in my Savior as my All in all,
> Standing on the promises of God.
>
> Standing, standing,
> Standing on the promises of God my Savior;
> Standing, standing,
> I'm standing on the promises of God.
>
> (*Hymns*, 340)

Moreover, we joyfully proclaim:

> How firm a foundation, ye saints of the Lord,
> Is laid for your faith in His excellent word!
> What more can He say than to you He hath said,
> To you who for refuge to Jesus have fled?
>
> (*Hymns*, 339)

CHAPTER FIVE

THE NEW COVENANT AND THE TESTAMENT

In chapter three we pointed out that in the new covenant there are promises as well as facts. We also pointed out that the word "testament" in Hebrews 9:16 is the same word for "covenant" in the original text. The covenant is referred to several times in the book of Hebrews. Indeed, we might say that Hebrews has this one specific purpose, that is, to tell us what the new covenant is. Hebrews, especially chapters six through thirteen, pays special attention to this matter. Now in this chapter we come to the matter of the new covenant and the testament, or will.

In Hebrews 9:15-17 it says, "And because of this He is Mediator of a new covenant, so that, death having taken place for redemption of the transgressions under the first covenant, those who have been called might receive the promise of the eternal inheritance. For where there is a testament there must of necessity be the death of him who made it. For a testament is confirmed where there has been death, since it has no force when he who made it is living." The word "Mediator" in verse 15 carries the meaning of one who acts as a guarantee so as to secure something which otherwise would not be obtained. In this sense, therefore, "Mediator" can also be translated "Executor." "Testament" in verses 16 and 17 is the same as "covenant." From these verses we see four important things: (1) a covenant as well as a testament, (2) the one who made the testament, or the Testator, (3) the Executor of the testament, and (4) the effectiveness of the testament.

A COVENANT AS WELL AS A TESTAMENT

Why do we say that the covenant is also the testament? Is it God or the Lord Jesus who made the covenant with us? According to God's Word, it is God who has made the covenant with us and not the Lord Jesus. God is the covenanting party who stands opposite to us. But it is the Lord Jesus who has accomplished the covenant, for this covenant was made with the Lord's blood. As far as God is concerned, He made a covenant with us; but as far as the Lord Jesus is concerned, it was through His death that He bequeathed an eternal inheritance to us (Heb. 9:15). Therefore, it is a testament, or a will. For a covenant to become effective, the death of the covenanting one is not required, but for a testament to become effective, the death of the testator is required. By this we see that it is God who made the covenant with us, but it is the Lord Jesus who through His death bequeathed the testament, the bequest, to us.

As far as the contents are concerned, the new covenant is the same as the testament. They are also the same as far as our inheritance is concerned, except that in the expression of it there are two sides: God's side and the Lord's side. As far as God is concerned, He has made a covenant with us; but as far as the Lord Jesus is concerned, He has left us a testament. We have said that the new covenant includes three major parts: the cleansing, life and power, and the inward knowledge. As far as God's making a covenant with us is concerned, it is God who promised to forgive our sins and cleanse us; it is God who promised to impart life and power to us; and it is also God who promised to give us the inward knowledge, the deeper knowledge, of Himself. But as far as the Lord Jesus leaving His testament is concerned, it is He who has left us with the cleansing which comes through the forgiveness of sins; it is He who has left us with life and power; and it is also He who has left us with the knowledge of God Himself.

THE LORD JESUS BEING THE TESTATOR

We pointed out before that the new covenant was mentioned as early as the time of Jeremiah. However, for several hundred years no attention was paid to this matter. Then suddenly one day it came up again. According to 1 Corinthians 11:23-25, on the night the Lord was betrayed He "took bread; and when he had given thanks, he brake it, and said, This is my body, which is for you: this do in remembrance of me. In like manner also the cup, after supper, saying, This cup is the new covenant in my blood." The new covenant here is the very glorious new covenant mentioned in the book of Jeremiah. Now, through the blood of the Lord Jesus, this covenant has become our inheritance so that we can enjoy all its contents. This shows us that the new covenant is the Lord's testament, or will. Our Lord is the Testator. He has given us the spiritual inheritance in His will. What He has given us are the items included in the new covenant and indicated in Hebrews 8:10-12. These are the things which the Lord has bequeathed to us in His will. When we inherit something through a will, we receive what we did not originally possess. Through the new covenant we received something which we did not work for, but which has been bequeathed to us by the Lord Jesus.

THE LORD JESUS BEING THE EXECUTOR
OF THE TESTAMENT

Our Lord is not only the Testator, but also the Executor of the testament, or will, for "He is Mediator of a new covenant" (Heb. 9:15). We said before that as the Mediator of the new covenant, He is also the Executor. We know that when writing a will it is important to have witnesses, but it is even more important to have one who can execute the will. When there is a will without an executor, the will remains idle. We praise God that the Lord Jesus is not only the One who made the will, but also the One who executes the will. As far as death is concerned, the Lord Jesus is the

Testator; but as far as resurrection is concerned, He is the Executor of the will. The Lord Jesus brought the blood into the Holy of Holies (Heb. 9:12), indicating that the Testator had died; then the Lord Jesus became the Mediator of the new covenant in the heavens, indicating that He is the One who has the power to execute the testament. Our Lord is truly worthy to be praised! He has obtained a more excellent ministry, for He has become the Executor of the better covenant (Heb. 8:6).

We are told in Hebrews 12:22-24 that we have "come to Mount Zion and to the city of the living God, heavenly Jerusalem, and to myriads of angels, to the universal gathering, and to the church of the firstborn ones who have been enrolled in the heavens, and to God the Judge of all, and to the spirits of just men who have been made perfect, and to Jesus, the Mediator of the new covenant, and to the blood of sprinkling, which speaks better than that of Abel." This passage tells us that we have not come to the mountain which can be touched (v. 18), but to Mount Zion, the gathering place for God, the angels, the resurrected just men, and the firstborn ones. This is also the place where the Lord Jesus is, He who is the Mediator of the new covenant. In the heavens the Lord is not only the High Priest, but also the Mediator, the Executor, of the new covenant, so that it may become effective in us. The Lord will insure that the effectiveness of this covenant established with His blood be realized in us, enabling us to have the life and power to submit to God, to have a deeper knowledge of God, and to have the forgiveness of sins with no accusation in our conscience. He is Mediator of these things. According to God's faithfulness and righteousness, this covenant is inviolable and irrevocable. According to the Lord's resurrection power, this covenant is forever effective. We must say, "Hallelujah! The Lord is the One who has left us with such a rich testament! He is also the One who has the power to execute the testament!"

THE EFFECTIVENESS OF THE TESTAMENT

Hebrews 9:16-17 tells us that "where there is a testament there must of necessity be the death of him who made it. For a testament is confirmed where there has been death, since it has no force when he who made it is living." One day our Lord told His disciples: "This cup is the new covenant in my blood" (Luke 22:20). This means that the One who made the will has died, and that the covenant has begun to become effective. When the Lord Jesus brought the blood into the Holy of Holies (Heb. 9:12), He was telling God that the One who made the testament had died. Even those of us who are living realize that the One who made the testament died, for whenever we eat the bread and drink the cup we show forth the Lord's death (1 Cor. 11:26). "Show" can also be translated "declare." Whenever we eat the bread and drink the cup, we declare that the Lord has died. The Testator has died, and now the testament, the will, has become effective.

It is the Executor's responsibility to make the will effective. We are entitled to every bequest in the will. If the Executor is faithful, we shall receive all the bequests in the will, but if the Executor is not faithful, we may not receive the bequests to which we are entitled. Since our Lord is a responsible Executor, we shall receive all the bequests in the testament. As we have mentioned before, what the Lord has bequeathed to us in His testament includes three major items: (1) cleansing which comes through the forgiveness of sins, (2) life and power, and (3) an inward knowledge of God. These three items comprise all the needs of our spiritual life. The Lord Jesus has died and risen again for us. He not only left us a testament; He is also the Executor of the testament. Therefore, we should no longer live a life of poverty, dryness, and impotence. We should receive by faith all that is included in the testament.

Have you ever considered that it is enough to be baptized once in our life, but that we frequently need the breaking of bread in remembrance of the Lord? During the time of the Apostles, the believers broke the bread in remembrance of the Lord on the first day of every week, because the cup is the cup of the new covenant (Luke 22:20; 1 Cor. 11:25). Every Lord's Day when we drink the cup, we know that we are standing upon a covenant. The Lord said, "This cup is the new covenant in my blood"; therefore, when we drink, what we see is not the grape juice or the wine itself, but a new covenant which the Lord established with His blood. The Lord wants us to drink all that He has given to us. Every Lord's Day we are reviewing this new covenant so that we may remember the Lord and receive all that is included in this cup. The Lord wants us to remember, every time we drink it, that God is bound by this covenant and that He delights to give us all that is promised in the covenant. The Lord wants us to remember that we can enjoy constantly all that is included in the new covenant. Whenever we remember the Lord before God, this is what He would have us see. Both the bread and the cup are for us to remember the Lord. The Lord is dealing with us according to the terms in the covenant. Therefore, when we remember the Lord, we are remembering Him in the covenant.

Whether the testament is effective or not does not depend upon our efforts, but has much to do with whether or not we know what the riches in the testament are and whether we can believe in the effectiveness of the testament and in the fact that the Lord Jesus is the Executor of the testament. Now we shall give some illustrations.

The Forgiveness of Sins

Take, for example, the forgiveness of sins. Some may think, "I have sinned; I must try to do my best and to do good until my sins can be forgiven. But I do not know how long it might take before the sins could be forgiven." Others may think, "I have sinned; I should pray again and again until one day I feel peace. Then my sins will be forgiven." But in both cases we must realize that this is something they are trying to do by themselves; this is not something the Lord has bequeathed to us in His testament.

We must realize that our sins are cleansed and forgiven not through the accumulation of good works, for doing good is merely our basic duty; neither does it depend upon our praying until God forgets our sins, for our sins can never be erased through our prayer; neither is the whole matter resolved by praying until we forget our sins. We must realize that the matter of our sins being cleansed and forgiven is not solved by any way other than the blood, for, "without shedding of blood there is no forgiveness" of sins (Heb. 9:22). It is the blood of the Lord Jesus which has solved the problem of our sins, and it is the blood of the Lord Jesus which cleanses us from all our sins (1 John 1:7). "If we confess our sins, he is faithful and righteous to forgive us our sins, and to cleanse us from all unrighteousness" (1 John 1:9). This is the testament and this is the new covenant. Can we believe this?

The Release from Sin

Concerning the matter of release from sin, Romans 6:14 says, "For sin shall not lord it over you, for you are not under law but under grace." Some say this: "Although the Scriptures declare this, yet I still feel as weak as water. Whenever I face temptation I always fail." People like this continually try to do something themselves and continually struggle. This is not a bequest they find in the testament; this is not the new covenant. If they see what the new covenant is, they will say: "Praise God, power does not come from me; power is a bequest from the Lord to me!" This is the testament and this is the new covenant. Can we believe this?

Knowing and Doing God's Will

Some may say, "How can I know God's will, and how

can I do God's will?" The answer is that both the ability to know God's will and the power to do God's will are bequests in the testament of the Lord Jesus. Everyone who belongs to the Lord should obey God's will. Everyone who belongs to the Lord not only has the potential for knowing God's will, but also has the potential for doing God's will, for the Lord has bequeathed to us in His testament the ability to know God, and He has also bequeathed to us the power to do God's will (Heb. 13:20-21). This is the testament and this is the new covenant. Can we believe it?

The eternal inheritance which the Lord has bequeathed to us is spiritual and cannot be exhausted in our lifetime. But today how many belonging to the Lord can say that they have been purified and that they no longer have any conscience of sins? (Heb. 10:2). How many can say that the Lord's law has been imparted into their mind and inscribed upon their heart, and that by the inner life and power they are able to do God's will and please Him? How many today can say that because of the Lord's anointing in us we by no means need man's teaching to know God? Brothers and sisters, we must all realize that the Lord through His blood established the new covenant and bequeathed the rich testament — the bequest — to us. He is also the Executor of this will. Therefore, if we can receive it by faith, we shall become rich and free.

"O Lord, may You cause each one of us to see what the testament, the new covenant, is so that You may be fully satisfied when You see the effectiveness of the covenant of Your blood."

Chapter Six

THE CHARACTERISTICS OF THE CONTENT
OF THE NEW COVENANT

I. CLEANSING

We will now look specifically at the characteristics of the content of the new covenant. We have seen in previous chapters that according to Hebrews 8:10-12 the contents of the new covenant include three major parts. According to God's eternal purpose, He first imparted His life and power into us; then He became our God in the law of life that we might be His people in the law of life, that we might have a deeper knowledge of Him, and that we might live Him out through us. Since forgiveness of sins is only a procedure by which to achieve His purpose, Scripture puts forgiveness of sins at the very end. However, according to our spiritual experience, we first obtain cleansing, that is, the cleansing which comes from forgiveness; then we become God's people in the law of life, and then we possess a deeper knowledge of God in an inward way.

Now let us look at the matter of forgiveness of sins. Hebrews 8:10 and 11 form one continuous thought, while verse 12 is another start. Notice the word "for" in verse 12. It says, "For I will be propitious to their unrighteousnesses, and their sins I will by no means remember anymore." The word "for" shows us that God's being propitious to our unrighteousnesses and no longer remembering our sins occurs before we receive the life. In other words, what is mentioned in verse 12 occurs before that which is mentioned in verses 10 and 11. For this reason, the first thing to see is how our sins are forgiven and cleansed according to the covenant.

The Two Aspects of Sin

According to the Scriptures, sin has two aspects: the nature of sin and the act of sin. The nature of sin is sin that dwells in man, mastering and governing him and inciting him to commit sins (Rom. 6:17; 7:20-21). Sinful acts are the sins which are manifested outwardly in our daily life. Concerning each of our sinful acts, whether small or great, hidden or deliberate, there is a charge against us before God. God has also passed judgment upon them (Rom. 1:32; 6:23). This causes our conscience to feel uneasy whenever we think of them. Whenever we are dominated by sin and struggle without release, we feel wretched within (Rom. 7:23-24). Therefore, the sinful acts need to be forgiven and cleansed, but we also need to be delivered and released from our sinful nature (Rom. 6:7, 22). Praise God, the blood of the Lord Jesus deals with the charges of sin against us before God and purifies our conscience (Matt. 26:28; Rev. 1:5; Heb. 9:14); and the cross of the Lord Jesus deals with our old man, delivering us from the power of sin and freeing us from sin itself (Rom. 6:6, 18). For this reason, when Romans 1 through 5:11 speaks of our sins before God, the blood is mentioned. When Romans 5:12 through chapter eight speaks of the sin that is in us, the same portion mentions the fact that our old man has been crucified with Christ to annul the body of sin that we may no longer serve sin as slaves. Now let us see that our sins need to be forgiven and how they are forgiven and cleansed.

Sins Need to be Forgiven

Without exception everyone who has truly been quickened will be conscious of his own sins. For example, when the prodigal son in Luke 15 came to himself, he felt that he had sinned against Heaven and against his father. A person who is truly enlightened by the Holy Spirit cannot help but condemn himself concerning sin (John 16:8). It is at this moment he needs God's forgiveness. As soon as he sees his sin, he will consider the charges of sin against him before God; he will consider the punishment which his sin deserves; he will consider the unceasing pains of hell; and he will also hope to have a way to be saved. Perhaps at this time the gospel is preached telling how the Lord Jesus was crucified on the cross and how He shed His precious blood for the forgiveness of sin (Matt. 26:28) that men might be washed of their sin (Rev. 1:5). When a person hears this gospel and believes, his sins are forgiven (Acts 10:43; 26:18) and his conscience is purified (Heb. 9:14).

Luke 7:36-50 shows that God's forgiveness may not mean much to a self-righteous Simon, but to a sinner who is considered "what manner of woman" (v. 39) by others, it is very much needed. All that this sinful woman had received her entire life was mockery and contempt. This only caused her to pity herself and feel ashamed of herself. But on this particular day there was One before her named Jesus, who appeared so holy and yet was so accessible — who even allowed her to stand behind Him weeping at His feet. Her weeping indicated several things: (1) her suffering because of sin, (2) the hidden story in her heart, (3) her helplessness, and (4) her hope for a Savior! However, her weeping did not obtain Simon's sympathy; it only caused him to be full of thought (v. 39). Weeping for sin simply could not be understood by a self-righteous person like Simon. But Jesus understood! First He corrected Simon; then He spoke on behalf of this weeping woman, saying that her many sins are forgiven (v. 47). Then speaking directly to the woman, He said, "Thy sins are forgiven. ... Thy faith hath saved thee; go in peace" (vv. 48, 50). This forgiveness to her was a great gospel! It enabled her to no longer feel sorry for herself, but rather to be full of peace. This forgiveness henceforth would become a gospel to many great sinners.

Mark 2:1-12 shows us that to those self-righteous scribes, God's forgiveness was mere empty doctrine. It only caused them to criticize and judge the Son of God regarding His authority to forgive sins (vv. 6-7). But to the man sick of palsy, who was carried by four men, it was really beneficial. How many times sin causes not only torment in our heart, but ruin in our bodies! We realize that many illnesses are results of natural causes, contagion, or overexhaustion. But the Scriptures also indicate that some illnesses are the result of committing sin (Mark 2:5; John 5:14). When illness results from committing sin, whether obvious or hidden, the one who commits the sin knows. When a person commits sin which results in some incurable disease, all he can do is regret it; there is nothing more to say. The Lord knew that with this man sick of palsy, the cause of his illness was sin. For this reason He first spoke to the sick man, "Son, thy sins are forgiven" (Mark 2:5). Then He said, "I say unto thee, Arise, take up thy bed, and go unto thy house" (v. 11). The sins were forgiven and the sickness was healed. What a great gospel this is! Henceforth, this forgiveness would become a great gospel to many who were sick because of sin.

The Security of Forgiveness

According to the experience of those who serve the Lord, the more one sees his sins in the light, the more sorrowful he feels for his sins and the more he senses the grace of forgiveness. With some, because they have sinned so much and so grievously, there is always the fear that God will not forgive them. Some who have been frequently troubled by their past sins and suffered overmuch have developed a weak conscience. Even though their sins have been forgiven, whenever they think of them they are still afraid, fearing they have not been forgiven. They may even feel that it is too cheap for God to have forgiven them. Those in such a condition with such an attitude must realize that the security of forgiveness has a firm

foundation. Such a one must take note of the following two
points:

1. Forgiveness is Based Upon God's Righteousness

Our God is not only a holy God (1 Pet. 1:16), but One
who loves righteousness and hates lawlessness (Heb. 1:9).
His holy nature does not allow Him to tolerate sin, and His
righteous attitude causes Him to judge sin. His Word says,
"The wages of sin is death" (Rom. 6:23). His Word also
says that "without shedding of blood there is no
forgiveness" (Heb. 9:22). Whenever we commit sin, God
must condemn us for our sin. According to God's nature He
is holy; therefore, He cannot tolerate sin. According to
God's way of doing things, He is righteous; therefore, He
must punish sin. In Himself God is also glorious; for this
reason sinners cannot approach Him. Those who do
approach Him will surely die. God deals with man
according to the principles of His holiness, His righteousness, and His glory. Therefore our sins are not forgiven
without passing God's judgment. He does not simply
disregard the charges of sin against us. He forgives us our
sins and no longer remembers them, because the Lord
Jesus has shed His blood (Matt. 26:28; Eph. 1:7).

Grace never reigns by itself; grace reigns through
righteousness (Rom. 5:21). Grace never comes to us
directly; grace comes to us through the cross. It is not that
God sees us repenting, feeling sorry, and weeping for our
sins, and because of this He has pity upon us and forgives
us. No, God never does this. First God judges our sins; then
He forgives us (Isa. 53:5, 10, 12). A certain common saying
goes, "Grace and righteousness never come hand in hand."
However, those who are taught by grace realize that God's
way of forgiving men their sins is perfect in both grace and
righteousness.

Not only is this God's way, but sometimes even His
redeemed ones may express a little shadow of the
perfection in both grace and righteousness. A girl high

school student tells the following story. Her principal was one who belonged to the Lord. One day someone broke a piece of furniture in the school. The principal (a woman) conducted an investigation, but no one would admit to having broken it. She tried to explain to the students that it was not right to break public things in the school, and that it was even worse to have broken it and lack the courage to admit it. While she was saying this, she was also crying. Then a student came forward to confess. But this student was too poor to pay the damages. The principal then took the money from her own pocket, paid for the damage the student had done, and also forgave her of her sin. Such a gracious and righteous attitude and conduct on the part of the principal not only caused the student to know sin, but also enabled her to know both grace and righteousness. This is only a little shadow of the perfection of both grace and righteousness being manifested through God's redeemed people.

On the day the Lord of holiness bore the sins of us all, He cried loudly saying, "My God, My God, why have You forsaken Me?" (Matt. 27:46). This was even more painful than the crown of thorns on His head and the wounds and stripes on His body. Isaiah 53:5 says, "He was wounded for our transgressions, he was bruised for our iniquities." Who says that forgiveness is cheap? Those who have been taught by grace sing with tears and thankfulness:

> The depth of all Thy suffering
> No heart could e'er conceive,
> The cup of wrath o'erflowing
> For us Thou didst receive;
> And, oh, of God forsaken
> On the accursed tree;
> With grateful hearts, Lord Jesus,
> We now remember Thee.

(Hymns, 213)

2. Forgiveness is the Characteristic of the New Covenant

Once again let us look at Hebrews 8:12: "For I will be propitious to their unrighteousnesses, and their sins I will by no means remember anymore." This is one of the blessings given to us in the new covenant. It refers to God's forgiving us our sins in Christ. God can be propitious to our unrighteousnesses because Christ has shed His blood for us. Not only is He propitious to our unrighteousnesses, but He by no means remembers our sins anymore. That God does not remember our sins means that He forgets them. God's forgetting of our sins is not that He hides His face or purposely ignores them, but that Christ's blood has blotted out the charges of sin against us and washed us from our sins (Isa. 44:22; Heb. 1:3; Rev. 1:5). Today God is confining Himself to the covenant; He is willing to be restricted by the covenant. When He said, "I will be propitious to their unrighteousnesses," He will do it; and when He said, "their sins I will by no means remember anymore," He will not remember. This is the new covenant, and this is the gospel.

How unfortunate it is that what God remembers we forget, and what God does not remember we continue to keep in mind! Some people keep thinking: "I have committed so many grievous sins — has God really forgiven them all? Does God really forget them?" Others think: "God has blotted out my sins, but the trace of the blot is still there. Whenever God sees it He will again remember what kind of sinner I am." Those who have such thoughts do not know what the new covenant is. Hence, they do not know how to enjoy the rights of the new covenant.

We must not forget that God's forgiveness of our sins and no longer remembering our sins is the fulfillment of the first item in the new covenant. God made a covenant and said, "I will be propitious to their unrighteousnesses, and their sins I will by no means remember anymore"

(Heb. 8:12). If God would not forgive our sins, we could speak to Him in this manner: "O God, You have made a covenant with us. You must forgive our sins. You must do according to Your covenant." God has made a covenant, and He must act according to it. He cannot forgive or refuse to forgive at will, for He has given us a pledge, namely, a covenant.

We are told in Hebrews 10:1-2 that "the law, having a shadow of the coming good things, not the image itself of the things, can never by the same sacrifices which they offer continually every year perfect those who draw near. Otherwise, would they not have ceased to be offered, because those serving, having once been purified, would have no longer any conscience of sins?" This means that enjoying a clean conscience and no longer feeling sin is not something which can be experienced by those who offer the blood of bulls and sheep. Only the blood of the Lord Jesus can enable a man to have such an experience. When God sees the blood of the Lord Jesus, He forgives our sins and by no means remembers them anymore. This is a characteristic of the new covenant. God's Word could not be more clear. If you are a person whose conscience is without rest, who feels his conscience still accusing him for past sins, we would advise you to sing the following hymn until you can say "amen" from your heart. Then you will begin to enjoy the blessing of the forgiveness of sins in the new covenant.

> Why should I worry, doubt and fear?
> Has God not caused His Son to bear
>   My sins upon the tree?
> The debt that Christ for me has paid,
> Would God another mind have made
>   To claim again from me?
>
> Redemption full the Lord has made,
> And all my debts has fully paid,
>   From law to set me free.
> I fear not for the wrath of God,

For I've been sprinkled with His blood,
It wholly covers me.

For me forgiveness He has gained,
And full acquittal was obtained,
All debts of sin are paid;
God would not have His claim on two,
First on His Son, my Surety true,
And then upon me laid.

So now I have full peace and rest,
My Savior Christ hath done the best
And set me wholly free;
By His all-efficacious blood
I ne'er could be condemned by God,
For He has died for me!

(*Hymns*, 1003)

Confession of Sin and Forgiveness

When a sinner knows that he is a sinner and believes in the Lord Jesus, his sins are forgiven. This is beyond doubt. The question is, after a person has believed in the Lord and received forgiveness, does he need to be forgiven further? In order to answer this question we must first consider three facts: (1) After a person is saved, he *should not* continue to live in sin (Rom. 6:1-2), and he *should not* commit sin again (John 5:14; 8:11). (2) There is still the possibility that a believer can commit sin (1 John 1:8, 10), and it is possible that a Christian can be overtaken in some offense and be tempted and fall (Gal. 6:1; 1 Cor. 10:12). There are the examples of Peter's hypocrisy in Antioch, Barnabas pretending with a group, and the brother in Corinth who committed fornication (Gal. 2:11-13; 1 Cor. 5:1-2, 5, 11). In the case of the brother who committed fornication, the consequence was very serious; on the one hand his body was corrupted, and on the other hand he was excommunicated by the church. (3) In 1 John 3:9 we read that "Whosoever is begotten of God doeth no sin, because his seed abideth in him: and he cannot sin, because he is begotten of God." This refers to the *habit and nature* of a regenerated person.

If we are clear concerning these three points, we will admit that the more fellowship we have with God and the more we walk in the light of God, the more we need forgiveness and cleansing. God is light; therefore to have fellowship with God means to be in the light. This is shown clearly in 1 John 1:5-7. How then can we obtain forgiveness? The answer is in 1 John 1:9, which says, "If we confess our sins, he is faithful and righteous to forgive us our sins, and to cleanse us from all unrighteousness." It is clear from this verse that if a believer commits sin, he needs to *confess* it in order to be forgiven. We must "confess our sins." If we *confess* our sins, God is faithful and righteous to forgive us our sins and to cleanse us from all unrighteousness.

We might ask what God's faithfulness is and what God's righteousness is. God's faithfulness refers to the words which He speaks, while God's righteousness refers to the way in which He does things. In speaking God is faithful, and in acting God is righteous. Since He has said that He will forgive us our sins, He surely will forgive us our sins. Since He has said that He will cleanse us from all unrighteousness, He surely will cleanse us from all unrighteousness. Since He sent His Son to die for our sins, He cannot help but cleanse and forgive us our sins. Therefore, if we confess our sins, we must, by taking hold of the covenant which He has made with us, expect Him to forgive and cleanse us.

The following is a true story. In a certain city there was a sister whose conscience continually accused her and gave her no rest. Whenever she saw a preacher she would say, "My sins are so grievous! I don't know if God has forgiven me or not." On one occasion when she said that, the preacher asked her to read 1 John 1:9 with him. Then he asked her, "Have you confessed your sins before God?" She replied, "Yes I have, and I do it quite often." "What

then does God's Word say?" he asked. She said, "God's
Word says that if we confess our sins He is faithful and
righteous to forgive us our sins and to cleanse us from all
unrighteousness." "Then," asked the preacher, "what do
you say?" She answered, "I do not know whether God has
forgiven me or not." After this manner they read and
questioned, read and questioned; and then they prayed.
She again confessed her sins before God. After the prayer
he again asked her, "Has God forgiven you your sins?"
She again replied, "I don't know." Then that preacher
spoke to her very seriously: "Do you think that God is a
liar?" She answered, "How dare I?" The preacher replied,
"Then if we confess our sins, what does God say He will
do? God says that He is faithful and righteous to forgive us
our sins and to cleanse us from all unrighteousness." At
this point she understood; she had peace in her conscience.
From that time until the day she slept in the Lord she
remained joyful. The Lord's Word truly enlightened and
comforted her.

Therefore, we must remember that forgiveness of sins is
something in the covenant. If we confess according to
God's Word, God will forgive us according to His covenant.
Brothers and sisters, do we dare ask God by holding on to
His Word, "O God, Your Word says that if we confess our
sins, You will forgive us our sins and cleanse us from all
unrighteousness"? We must realize that God has made a
covenant with us so that we may speak to Him according
to His covenant. He wants us to ask by faith that He fulfill
what is in the covenant. We are not just asking God to
show us mercy; we are claiming our portion according to
the covenant. Praise God, even the forgiveness of sins is a
part of the new covenant.

Some no doubt think that if they really hate sin, it will
be easier for them to be forgiven. Others feel that if they
continue to feel sorrowful and have a contrite heart, it will
be easier for them to be forgiven. This kind of supposition
is utterly wrong. This is not what God's Word says. A

contrite heart and feelings of sorrow are a natural result, a natural attitude, issuing from enlightenment; it is not a condition we exchange for forgiveness. In the book, *The Christian's Secret of a Happy Life,* we read of a little girl who was asked, "If you commit sins, how will the Lord Jesus treat you and what will you do?" She said, "I will confess my sins to the Lord; the Lord Jesus will make me feel sorry for a while, and then He will forgive me." Do not think that these are only the words of a little child; this is also the story of many adults. Many grown-ups feel the same way. They think that after they confess their sins they need to feel sorry for a while; they need to wait until their heart feels no pain — then they will receive the evidence of forgiveness. Those who think in this way do not know what the new covenant is.

We must realize that forgiveness of sins is something in the new covenant, that because the Lord Jesus shed His blood, God must forgive us our sins and cleanse us from all unrighteousness. The moment we accept the Lord, God forgives us according to what He has said in the covenant; the moment we confess our sins, at that very moment God forgives us according to what is stated in the covenant. God is bound by the covenant He has made with us. We need only ask God to act according to what is stated in the covenant, and He is bound to do it.

We must remind the reader that the confession referred to here is something we do after seeing sin in God's light. God's light does not tolerate sin. When a person truly sees sin in God's light, condemns sin as sin, and comes to God to confess his sin, God will forgive such a person's sin and cleanse his unrighteousness. Some people take shelter in the confession of sin: day by day they continue to speak lies under the precious blood, and day by day they continue to lose their temper under the precious blood — this is definitely wrong. To them confession is a formula and a method. On one hand they commit sins, and on the other hand they confess as a formality. This is not confession in

God's light. Such confession is only confession in words. We should never practice this. What we are saying here is that the more we fellowship with God, the more we walk in the light of life, the easier it is for us to see sins; then we realize how much we need God's forgiveness and the cleansing of the precious blood. It is this kind of confession which counts. With this confession we enjoy the rest issuing from the forgiveness of sins mentioned in the new covenant.

Revelation 4:3 says that there is a rainbow around the throne. The rainbow is the sign of the covenant which God made with Noah. It means that God has never forgotten that covenant. It also means that God must listen to man's prayer if he prays according to the covenant. As long as the rainbow is around the throne, God must listen to the prayer which is according to the covenant. God has pledged Himself to us in this way that we may pray to Him according to the covenant. What a wonderful grace this is!

Who today has not yet solved the problem of sins? You can bring your sins before God, holding on to God's Word and believing Him according to His covenant. Then you can rest in His covenant. The reason we have lost so many spiritual blessings is that we have not realized that God has made a covenant with us. God has made a covenant with us that we may speak to Him according to the covenant. Then He will act according to the covenant.

CHAPTER SEVEN

THE CHARACTERISTICS OF THE CONTENT OF THE NEW COVENANT

II. LIFE AND POWER

We have seen previously that in the new covenant the forgiveness of sins is the gospel of grace. If a man can believe this grace for the forgiveness of his sins, his conscience will have rest. We know that many who belong to the Lord have received this grace for the forgiveness of their sins. Concerning this aspect of the new covenant they not only believe, but they are also willing to testify that God has forgiven them their sins and cleansed them from all their unrighteousnesses.

However, in addition to this aspect of the new covenant concerning the forgiveness of sins, there are also two other extremely glorious and precious parts of the new covenant: one is the matter of life and power, and the other is the matter of the inward knowledge, or knowing God in an inward way. These two aspects have been much neglected, and are not understood or even believed by many. This is why so many of God's children are so spiritually poverty-stricken. This is also why many are so weak and full of failure. Brothers and sisters, it is good that God has forgiven us our sins, but if after our sins are forgiven we remain the same, God is still unable to obtain in us what He intends, and we still cannot do God's will. In that case, what is the difference between us and the children of Israel who wandered in the wilderness? And if there is no difference, where is the glory of the new covenant? Therefore, brothers and sisters, we must see this better aspect of the new covenant.

According to Hebrews 8:9, under the old covenant God took the children of Israel by their hand and led them out of Egypt, but in the new covenant God draws our hearts out of Egypt. In the old covenant God gave the law externally to the children of Israel, but in the new covenant God has put the law inside of us and has inscribed it upon our hearts. Under the old covenant, there were those who taught the children of Israel, yet they observed God's works for forty years and were always going astray in their hearts; they did not know God's ways (Heb. 3:9-10). However in the new covenant there is no need to be taught by man, for all can know God in an inward way from the least to the greatest. Now let us see how it is that God has put His law into us and inscribed it upon our hearts, and why it is an extremely glorious and precious part of the new covenant.

Before we begin, we must read the related verses. The first is Hebrews 8:10: "For this is the covenant which I will covenant with the house of Israel after those days, says the Lord: I will impart My laws into their mind, and on their hearts I will inscribe them, and I will be God to them, and they shall be a people to Me." Another is Hebrews 10:16: "This is the covenant which I will covenant with them after those days, says the Lord: I will put My laws upon their hearts and upon their minds I will inscribe them." These two verses both speak first of imparting or of inscribing. They are different in this respect: in 8:10 the mind is first mentioned and then the heart, while in 10:16, the heart is mentioned first and then the mind. Whether the mind or the heart is mentioned first, both passages speak of imparting or inscribing, and both mention the mind and the heart. Therefore both speak of the same thing. We must also realize that both these passages are quotations from Jeremiah 31:33, which reads: "But this is the covenant that I will make with the house of Israel after those days, saith Jehovah: I will put my law in their inward parts, and in their heart will I write it; and I will be their God, and they shall be my people."

Ezekiel 36:25-28 speaks of the same thing as Jeremiah 31:31-34, except that some words are clearer in Ezekiel while other words are clearer in Jeremiah. The passage in Ezekiel reads: "And I will sprinkle clean water upon you, and ye shall be clean: from all your filthiness, and from all your idols, will I cleanse you. A new heart also will I give you, and a new spirit will I put within you; and I will take away the stony heart out of your flesh, and I will give you a heart of flesh. And I will put my Spirit within you, and cause you to walk in my statutes, and ye shall keep mine ordinances, and do them. And ye shall dwell in the land that I gave to your fathers; and ye shall be my people, and I will be your God."

At least five things are referred to in these verses: 1) cleansing with clean water, 2) giving a new heart, 3) giving a new spirit, 4) taking away the stony heart and giving a heart of flesh, and 5) having His Spirit within. When we put these five matters together, the result is to "cause you to walk in my statutes, and ye shall keep my ordinances and do them ... and ye shall be my people, and I shall be your God." Notice the word "cause" in verse 27; it means to motivate. The Holy Spirit who indwells us gives us new strength to do God's will and to please God, so that God can be our God and we can be His people.

REGENERATION

When speaking of how God has put His law within us and has inscribed it upon our hearts, we must start from regeneration, for regeneration means that the Holy Spirit has put the uncreated life of God into man's spirit. Regeneration is a new thing that takes place in man's spirit; therefore regeneration is not a matter of behavior but a matter of life.

Man's Creation

Before we can speak adequately of regeneration we must say something regarding the creation of man. We read in Genesis 2:7 that "Jehovah God formed man of the dust of the ground, and breathed into his nostrils the breath of life; and man became a living soul." The breath of life mentioned here is the spirit, the source of man's life. The Lord said, "It is the Spirit Who gives life" (John 6:63a). Job also said, "The breath of the Almighty giveth me life" (Job 33:4). In this verse the word "life" in Hebrew is in the plural form. When God so breathed into man He produced two lives, one spiritual and one soulish. When God breathed the breath of life into man's body, it became the spirit; and at the same time, when this spirit came into contact with the body, it produced the soul. This is the way in which the spiritual life and the soulish life originated in man. It becomes clear, then, that man is composed of three parts: the spirit, the soul, and the body.

The New Testament also shows that man is tripartite. For example, there is a verse which says, "May your spirit and soul and body be preserved entire" (1 Thes. 5:23). There is another verse which says, " ... even to the dividing of soul and spirit, both of joints and marrow ... " (Heb. 4:12). These verses show us that man is of three parts: spirit and soul and body.

The body is the seat of world-consciousness; the soul is the seat of self-consciousness; and the spirit is the seat of God-consciousness. Through the physical body we have communication with the physical world by means of the five senses. For this reason it is called the sense of the world. The soul, including the mind, emotion, and will, constitutes man's self, man's personality. Hence, we call the soul the sense of the self. The spirit, which includes the faculties of the conscience, intuition, and fellowship, knows how to worship God, how to serve God, and how to enter into relationship with God. Therefore, the function of the spirit is to have the sense of God.

Through the soul, the spirit controls man's whole being. Whenever the spirit wants to do something, it passes its intention on to the soul, and the soul exercises the body to obey the command from the spirit. According to God's arrangement, the human spirit is the highest part of man and should rule his whole being. Yet, the will is the most prominent part of man's personality and belongs to the soul. The will of man is also able to make its own choice. It can choose whether to be ruled by the spirit, by the body, or by the self. Because the soul is so powerful and occupies the seat of personality, the Scriptures call man "a living soul."

God's Purpose in Creating Man

We have said repeatedly that God has an eternal purpose, which is to dispense Himself into man. His delight is to enter into man and become one with man so that man may have His life and nature. He created man, Adam, and put him into the Garden of Eden. In the midst of that garden the tree of life and the tree of the knowledge of good and evil (Gen. 2:9). Those two trees were the most conspicuous and drew man's attention. Concerning the trees in the garden God said, "Of every tree of the garden thou mayest freely eat: but of the tree of the knowledge of good and evil, thou shalt not eat of it: for in the day that thou eatest thereof thou shalt surely die" (Gen. 2:16-17). On the other hand He implied that the fruit of the tree of life could be eaten. Had man eaten of the fruit of the tree of life, he would have chosen God, for the tree of life signifies God Himself. Oh, the God of creation — His purpose toward man is so wonderful and good!

Originally man was made by God (Gen. 2:7); man's original life was made by God also. As far as man's original created life was concerned, it was upright (Eccl. 7:29) and it was good (Gen. 1:31). But as far as God's eternal purpose, man had not yet received the uncreated life of God. Therefore man still needed to choose God and

God's life. In Greek there are three different words, all of which translate into the one English word, life. One of these words is *bios*. It refers to life in the flesh. The Lord Jesus spoke of the widow who put all her living into the treasury (Luke 21:4); the word translated living is from the word *bios*. The second Greek word is the word *psuche*. *Psuche* refers to man's natural life, which is the soul-life. When the Scriptures speak specifically of man's life, this is the word used (Matt. 16:26; Luke 9:24). The third word for life is *zoe*. *Zoe* is the highest life, the spiritual life, and the uncreated life. When the Scriptures speak of eternal life, as in John 3:16, the word used is *zoe*.

Man's Fall

However, the man Adam did not choose life. He sinned and became fallen by eating the fruit of the tree of the knowledge of good and evil which God forbade him to eat. Before that time it was possible for man's spirit to have fellowship with God, but after man fell, his spirit became estranged from God (Eph.4:18) and dead to God (Col. 2:13; Eph. 2:1). God told Adam from the beginning that the day he ate of the tree of knowledge of good and evil he would surely die (Gen. 2:17). As far as Adam's flesh was concerned, after he ate the fruit of the tree of knowledge of good and evil, he lived for several hundred years (Gen. 5:3-5). Therefore, the death spoken of here implies that the spirit will die before the flesh expires. Death simply means to be estranged from life, and, as we know, God is a God of life. By being estranged from God, Adam was estranged from life. We know that Adam's spirit died. This does not mean that his spirit disappeared, but that his spirit lost its fellowship with God; it lost its keen sense. When Adam's spirit died it was still there but it was dead to God. Adam had lost the function of his spirit. After man fell, he became dominated by his soul and was fleshly (Rom. 7:14). He could no longer understand the things of God (1 Cor. 2:14). Man also was not subject to the law of God, neither could he be. Furthermore, according to Romans 8:7-8, man in the flesh cannot please God.

Taking these facts into account, does this mean that God's eternal purpose will not be accomplished? No! God is God! He has planned according to His good pleasure and He will accomplish His eternal will and fulfill His eternal purpose. He still desires to dispense His own life to man, enter into man, and be one with man. To do this He has to solve the problem of man's sin and redeem fallen man; He has to release His life through His Son, and He has to regenerate man through the Holy Spirit.

The Way of God's Salvation

In order to deal with man's sin and bring fallen man back to Himself, God sent Christ. Christ Himself bore our sins in His body on the cross, "that we, having died unto sins, might live unto righteousness" (1 Pet. 2:24). This was typified in Numbers 21:4-9, when Moses lifted up the brass serpent in the wilderness. The children of Israel had committed sin and deserved death, but God told Moses to lift up the brass serpent so that those who had been bitten by the serpent might look upon it and live. In the same manner Christ was also lifted up. He died for us and bore our sins. Now we who were dead in sin may have God's life and live (John 3:14-15).

God desires to release His life, so for that purpose He put His life in Christ (John 1:4; 1 John 5:11). The life of God which is in Christ was released when Christ died on the cross, for Christ is the grain of wheat which fell into the earth and died (John 12:24). When Christ died, God's life was released. It is also true that God regenerated us through the resurrection of Jesus Christ from the dead (1 Pet. 1:3).

Regeneration means to be born of God (John 1:13), to be born of heaven (1 Cor. 15:47). Regeneration also means to be born of the water and of the Spirit (John 3:5). Concerning this we need some explanation. When John the

Baptist came preaching and baptizing, he said, "I baptized you in water; but he shall baptize you in the Holy Spirit" (Mark 1:8). John the Baptist put water and the Holy Spirit together, and the Lord Jesus also put water and the Holy Spirit together. The water to which John referred is the water of baptism; hence, the water to which the Lord Jesus referred must also be the water of baptism. The words spoken to Nicodemus by the Lord Jesus must have been words which could be easily understood. At that time many knew that John baptized with water; so when the Lord Jesus mentioned water, Nicodemus would readily understand that this referred to the water of baptism practiced by John. If the water mentioned by the Lord Jesus had implied something else, it would have been difficult for Nicodemus to understand. The water spoken of, therefore, must have referred to the water of baptism.

The baptism which John practiced was the baptism of repentance. He told people that they should believe on Him that should come after him, that is, on Jesus (Acts 19:4). The baptism of repentance which John performed could not cause men to be regenerated. To be regenerated, one must be born both of water and of the Holy Spirit. The baptism of repentance means not only that man's actions are evil and dead and he needs to repent; it means also that man himself is corrupt and dead and needs to be buried, that is, to be baptized. When a man goes down into the water to be baptized, he admits before God that his actions are evil and confesses that his whole being is corrupt and dead in sin; therefore he deserves only death and burial.

But man is not born merely "of water." He must be born "of water and of the Spirit." He must also receive the Holy Spirit which the Lord Jesus gives in order to obtain God's life. John the Baptist came preaching "Repent!" (Mark 1:4), to which the Lord Jesus immediately added, "Believe" (Mark 1:15). Repentance causes man to leave all that is of himself, while believing causes man to enter into all that is of God. Because of repentance man enters into the water, and because of faith he enters into the Holy Spirit. By entering into the water and the Spirit, he is born of water and of the Spirit. Through repentance we enter into the water and terminate the life of the old man. By believing we enter into the Holy Spirit and obtain God's life. This is regeneration.

Although regeneration is to be "born of water and of the Spirit," the work which brings a man subjectively to regeneration is accomplished completely by the Holy Spirit. (Objectively, it is accomplished completely by Christ.) Therefore, in John 3 the Lord Jesus spoke only once of being "born of water," while he mentioned being "born of the Spirit" three times (vv. 5, 6, 8). Regeneration means that we have been "born of the Spirit." The Spirit comes to "convict the world concerning sin" (John 16:8) and cause man to repent; He leads man to receive the Lord Jesus by faith; He then enters into such a believer who has repented and imparts God's life to him that he might be regenerated. The Spirit enlightens man, causes him to repent, leads him to believe, and causes him to receive God's life. He does all this by using the words in the Scripture, that is, by means of the word of truth of the gospel. Therefore the Scriptures say that God regenerates us by the gospel and by the word of truth (1 Cor. 4:15; James 1:18). We have been "begotten again, not of corruptible seed, but of incorruptible, through the word of God, which liveth and abideth" (1 Pet. 1:23). Through the Spirit and by the use of His words, God imparted and sowed His life into us. Because the Holy Spirit touched us, we believed God's words, and God's life entered into us. God's life is embodied in His words. Moreover, God's words are life (John 6:63). Therefore, when we receive God's words, we receive God's life.

The life which we receive at the time of regeneration is not fleshly life, but spiritual. Like the wind, this life is without form and cannot be seen (John 3:8). Yet it is very practical and can be realized by man. Therefore, regeneration is simply this: that in addition to his own life, man receives the life of God.

When we are regenerated, we have "authority to become children of God" (John 1:12), and we are related to God in life as a son to his father (Gal. 4:6; Rom. 8:15-16). God's uncreated life is God's life and also "eternal life" (John 17:3). It is the life which Adam could have obtained but did not. It is the life which man does not have before regeneration, but which enters into us at the time of regeneration. This is the characteristic of the new covenant, the glory of the new covenant. Hallelujah!

In God's life is God's nature. Therefore, when we have God's life, we become "partakers of the divine nature" (2 Pet. 1:4). We can understand God's heart, we spontaneously desire to do what God desires to do, and it is possible for us to live out God's image (Col. 3:10). If a man says that he has received the life of the Son of God and yet does not in the least live out the nature of this life, neither does he love righteousness nor hate sin, then this man's faith and regeneration are doubtful. God's nature is in God's life. If we are without the nature of God's life, how can we say that we have God's life?

"The spirit of man is the lamp of Jehovah" (Prov. 20:27). After Adam's fall, man's spirit became darkened. When the Holy Spirit regenerated us and put God's life into us, He made our spirit alive (Eph. 2:5). It was like lighting a lamp. The first part of man to die at the time of Adam's fall was the human spirit; therefore, at the time of regeneration, when the Holy Spirit puts God's uncreated life into man's spirit, the first part of man to become alive is his spirit. The work of the Holy Spirit starts from within man, working from the center to the circumference, from the spirit to the soul, and then to the body. When the Holy Spirit regenerates man, it is something done completely in the human spirit. In the past, our spirit died because of sin. Now the spirit has become alive (Col. 2:13), and we can know God and be sensitive to sin. For this reason, if a man says that he is regenerated, yet has no knowledge of God and no feeling concerning sin, his regeneration is doubtful.

When the Holy Spirit regenerated us, He gave us a "new heart" and a "new spirit" (Ezek. 36:26). For the Lord to give us a new heart does not mean that He has given us another heart, but that He has renewed our corrupted heart. In like manner, for God to give us a new spirit does not mean that He gives us another spirit, but that He enlivens our deadened spirit and renews our old spirit. A new heart enables us to think of God, desire God, and love God. A new heart enables us to have new desires and new inclinations toward heavenly and spiritual things. With a new spirit we are not weak and impotent toward spiritual things as before, and we are no longer ignorant of the things of God. With a new spirit, we become strong and powerful concerning spiritual things, we obtain understanding regarding the things of God (1 Cor. 2:12), and we have fellowship with God.

Another glorious thing which happens when we are regenerated is that God puts His Spirit within our spirit (Ezek. 36:27). After regeneration the Spirit indwells our renewed spirit. This is something the people under the old covenant knew nothing of. In the old covenant time the Holy Spirit of God did work upon man, but the Scriptures never say clearly that God's Spirit came to dwell in man forever. How do we know that in the new covenant time the Holy Spirit dwells in us continually? We know this by the word the Lord told His disciples: "And I will ask the Father and He will give you another Comforter, that He may be with you forever; even the Spirit of reality, Whom the world cannot receive, because it does not behold Him or know Him; but you know Him, because He abides with you and shall be in you" (John 14:16-17). The Comforter is really the Lord Himself coming in a different form, for the Lord continued: "I will not leave you orphans; I am coming to you" (v.18). "He" in verse 17 is "I" in verse 18. Therefore the Comforter is the Lord Himself coming in another form. When the Lord was on the earth He was with His disciples all the time, but He could not dwell in them. After resurrection, the Lord became a life-giving Spirit. Hence, He could dwell in them. As God incarnate, Christ in the flesh could only be in the midst of men, but Christ as the Spirit can enter into men. Therefore, when the Spirit is in us, it is Christ in us (Rom. 8:9-10; 2 Cor. 13:5); and when Christ is in us, it is God in us (the Christ in Ephesians 3:17 is the God in v. 19). What a blessed thing it is that the Creator dwells in His creatures. This is the most wonderful, the most blessed, and the most glorious thing in the whole universe!

The Lord did not leave us orphans. This means that He Himself will take care of us, nourish us, nurture and edify us, and bear all our responsibilities. What Christ accomplished on the cross is objective, but the Spirit indwelling us turns the objective facts into our subjective experience. The Spirit of reality guides man into all the reality.

The word "comforter" in Greek has two meanings: one is "the helper who stands by." This speaks of the Holy Spirit being our available Helper. Whenever we need His help it seems He is beside us and is ready to help us. The second meaning is "advocate." Christ pleads our cause before God for our benefit.

When we were regenerated, we became a saved person. Moreover, when God saved us, it was through the washing of regeneration (Titus 3:5). Regeneration not only caused us to have life, but also washed us. Through regeneration our old creation was washed away. This means that we are saved and delivered from the old creation. We were originally an old creation, but now through the renewing of the Holy Spirit (Titus 3:5) we have a new heart, a new spirit, and an uncreated life. "If any man is in Christ, he is a new creature: the old things are passed away; behold, they are become new" (2 Cor. 5:17).

When man has God's life, he can know God and understand spiritual things. Today, spiritually, he is in the kingdom of God; in the future, in reality, he will enter into the kingdom of God (John 3:3, 5).

Through regeneration we not only have God's life today, but also a living hope for the future. We have an inheritance incorruptible and undefiled that does not fade away, reserved in heaven for us (1 Pet. 1:3-4). Upon the earth today we are a heavenly people, and in the future we shall enjoy the heavenly portion.

We can praise and thank God that regeneration is so wonderful and that its results are so blessed and glorious. We must sing:

> O what a mystery, the Savior
>   With me is one!
> O what a marvelous salvation
>   God gives me in His Son!
> Hallelujah! Hallelujah!
>   Glorious mystery!
> Nothing in heaven or earth can sever
>   Jesus my Lord from me!
>   (*Hymns*, 1074)

When we were regenerated we became God's kind. But we still need to grow up to maturity that we may be like His kind, that is, that we may become a glorified God-man. We must realize that every life has its own characteristic and ability. For instance, the birds have the bird life with its characteristic and ability. Birds like to fly and have the ability to fly. The fish have the fish life with the characteristic and ability of the fish life. The fish life enjoys living in the water and possesses the ability to live in water. Not only is the animal life like this, but the plant life as well. "Every good tree produces goodly fruit, but the corrupt tree produces evil fruit. A good tree cannot bear evil fruit, neither can a corrupt tree bear goodly fruit" (Matt. 7:17-18). This is the spontaneity of life; this is the law of life.

Since we were regenerated we have God's life. This life

also has its characteristic and ability. However, we must realize that, although this life which we have obtained is complete, it has not matured. The organism of this life is complete; it can reach the highest level. However, when we were regenerated, what we experienced was just a new birth. The life we received was not yet grown up and matured. It was like fruit whose life is complete yet immature. The new birth is complete in organism but not in maturity. Only maturity can bring completeness to every part of the organism. Therefore, after regeneration man needs a long process of renewal by the Holy Spirit until this life is perfected in every part of his being. In later paragraphs we shall see point by point how this seed of life manifests its character and ability.

THE LAW OF LIFE

Let us read Hebrews 8:10 again: "I will impart My laws into their mind, and on their hearts I will inscribe them." This verse shows the difference between the new covenant and the old. In the old covenant the law was placed outside of man and written on tables of stone. In the new covenant the law is put inside of man and inscribed upon his heart. That which was placed outside of man and written upon tables of stone must be of the letter (2 Cor. 3:6). In that case, what is the law that can be put inside of us and inscribed upon our hearts? And what is the nature of this law? From God's Word we see that the law which can be imparted into us and inscribed upon the heart is not the law of letters, but the law of life. Not every law is necessarily of life, but every life must have a law. The law which God imparted into us comes from the life which God imparted into us. Since we have the life of God, we must also have the law of God's life. God came into the world in His Son, and the Son of God enters into man through the Spirit. The Spirit causes man to have life. This life has its function in man, and this function is the law of life we are referring to here. In other words, this law of life comes from the Spirit. This is what is mentioned in Romans 8:2: "the law of the Spirit of life." Note that this law is singular. In the old covenant there were many laws, but in the new covenant there is not the first law, the second, the third, and the last. In the new covenant there is only *one* law, the law of life. This is the new covenant.

Here we must point out that the nature of the law of life is that it has a spontaneous function. For example, your ears can spontaneously hear — there is no need to regulate them with effort. Likewise, with the eyes, there is no need to make special effort to regulate them. The eyes see spontaneously. With the tongue you need not use your strength to regulate it. When it tastes anything bad, you spontaneously spit it out; when it tastes anything good, you spontaneously swallow it. If the ears cannot hear, the eyes cannot see, and the tongue cannot taste properly, it is due either to some physical illness or the absence of life. What God has imparted into us is life, and this life has a law; God has not put some kind of regulations or letters into us, but something living. It is the law of life; it is something spontaneous.

The following example will illustrate the point. Suppose you say to a dead peach tree, "You should have green leaves, you should have pink flowers, and in due time you should bear peaches." You may speak to it in this manner from the beginning of the year to the end, but you will be speaking in vain and asking in vain, for it is dead — it does not have life. If, however, your peach tree is living, you need not say anything. Spontaneously it will bud, grow leaves, blossom, and eventually bear fruit. This is the law of life. This law has its spontaneous function.

Since what God has imparted into us is life, the law of the life must also be there. It must have its spontaneous function. This law will spontaneously live out the life in us, and this life will naturally bring forth the content of this life through the law. Moreover, this life will manifest God's wisdom and all that He is through this law. As long as we do not hinder it, it will spontaneously come forth.

THE LAWS AND THE INWARD PARTS

Jeremiah 31:33 says, "I will put my law in their inward parts, and in their heart will I write it." In order to understand what the inward parts are, we must consider the composition of the heart. The heart we are considering here is not the biological heart, but the heart referred to in the Scriptures and known in the experience of many who belong to the Lord. According to the scriptural record, the heart includes several parts. We shall now consider them one by one.

The Parts of the Heart

(1) The heart includes the conscience. We see this in Hebrews 10:22 which says, "Having our hearts sprinkled from an evil conscience...." First John 3:20 says, "If our heart condemns us...." To condemn is the function of the conscience, and we see from these verses that the conscience is within the system of the heart. For this reason we say that the heart includes the conscience.

(2) The heart includes the mind. In Matthew 9:4 we read: "Why are you thinking evil things in your hearts?" Mark 2:6 speaks of reasoning in the heart; Luke 1:51 speaks of the imagination of the heart; and Luke 24:38 of the questionings of the heart. Understanding also takes place in the heart (Matt. 13:15). Mary kept certain sayings and pondered them in her heart (Luke 2:19), and according to Hebrews 4:12, thoughts are in the heart. From these verses we can see clearly that the heart includes the mind.

(3) The heart includes the will. Acts 11:23 has this phrase: "with purpose of heart"; Romans 6:17 mentions having "obeyed out from the heart"; 2 Corinthians 9:7 says that one can purpose in his heart; and Hebrews 4:12 speaks of the "intents of the heart." These verses show us clearly that the heart includes the will.

(4) The heart also includes the emotion. Genesis 45:26 says that "Jacob's heart fainted." Luke 24:32 says, "did not our heart burn within us?" John 14:1 says, "Let not your heart be troubled"; and in 16:22 it says, "your heart will rejoice." These verses indicate clearly that the heart includes the emotion.

Although we dare not say that the conscience is the heart, that the mind is the heart, that the will is the heart, or that the emotion is the heart, we can say that the heart includes the conscience, the mind, the will, and the emotion. The heart controls the conscience, the mind, the will, and the emotion, and is the totality of these four aspects of our being. Later, when we mention the specific parts of the heart, we will refer to them as the conscience of the heart, the mind of the heart, the will of the heart, and the emotion of the heart.

From this we can see that the inward parts mentioned in Jeremiah 31:33 include at least the four parts of the heart: the conscience, the mind, the will, and the emotion.

The Relationships Between the Heart and the Laws

In Hebrews 8:10 and 10:16 we have the plural word laws, although the law of life is singular not plural. Why then in these two verses does it say laws? Why has the law become plural? The reason is that the life which we have received through regeneration has only one law. This is the law of life itself. But this law has more than one function in us. God's life in each of our inner parts has its function. In the spirit it has its function; in the mind it has its function; in the will it also has its function, as well as in the emotion. In all the inward parts it has its function. When Jeremiah says that "I will put my law into their inward parts," it means that the law of God's life in each of the inward parts has its function.

Therefore, as far as the law itself is concerned, it is singular; but concerning the function of this law in our being, it is plural. It is just like running water; the source is one, but the pipes are many. Life has only one law in us, but this law has spread to our inward parts. We have this law in our spirit, in our mind, in our will, and also in our emotions. As far as life itself is concerned there is one law, but as far as the function of its operation is concerned there are many laws. The law spreads into the different parts and becomes several laws, but the source is one.

The Heart Being the Gate of Our Being

Although the spirit is the highest part of man, what represents man's self is not the spirit but the heart. It is the heart which represents man. Psalm 4:4 speaks of communing with your own heart. This indicates that the heart is man's true self. Our heart is the most important part of our being.

The heart is between the spirit and the soul. Therefore all that enters into the spirit must pass through the heart, and all that comes forth from the spirit must also pass through the heart. Proverbs 4:23 says, "Keep thy heart with all diligence; for out of it are the issues of life." This means that the heart is the exit through which the life flows out. In other words, the fruit which man produces outwardly comes out of his heart, and for this reason the heart is the most important thing. The heart is the necessary path through which the life moves. Therefore, before God's life enters into us, what must be touched first is our heart. If our heart has not become sorrowful and has not yet repented, God's life cannot enter. Whether God causes us to feel the sufferings of sin, the sweetness of His love, or the preciousness of Christ, He always does it by touching our heart, causing us to feel sorrowful and bringing us to repentance. The sorrowfulness of the heart is the specific function of the conscience, and being repentant is the turning of the mind. When our heart is thus touched, our will decides and our heart believes. By this receiving of Christ, the life of God enters into us and is planted within us (1 Pet. 1:23).

The Heart is the Switch of Life

A grain of wheat planted into the earth will begin to grow and continue to grow. However, its growth does require certain conditions. For instance, if the seed is planted but is never watered, its growth will be hindered. We see this same principle not only in life, but also in physics. Electricity is powerful, but when the little switch is turned off, the flow of electricity is stopped. It is true that life is powerful and spontaneous, but if there is something hindering its development or if the conditions for its development are absent, it will not grow. It will appear as if the growth has stopped.

How then can this life develop within us? We must remember that the receiving of life begins with our heart and that the growth of this life also begins with our heart. Whether the life within us can grow depends upon whether our heart is open toward God. If our heart is open toward God, the life in us will grow and spread; but if our heart is closed toward God, the life in us will not be able to develop and spread out. Therefore, the growth and development of life in us is entirely a matter of the heart. We must not ignore this matter.

We must realize that the heart has desires and inclinations, while the spirit enables us to have fellowship and communion with God. Therefore, to desire God and love God is not a matter of the spirit, but a matter of the heart; whereas, to worship and serve God is not a matter of the heart, but a matter of the spirit. The heart can love God, but it cannot touch God. The heart can incline to God, but cannot have fellowship with God. Only the spirit can touch God and have fellowship with God.

Some would say that if we wish to touch the things of God we need to use our mind, just as when we hear sounds we need to use our mind. While it is true that to hear sounds we must use our mind, it is also true that to hear sounds we must use our ears. If someone is speaking yet

you do not have ears, your mind cannot understand what
is being said. The same is true with seeing; if there are red,
white, yellow, and blue colors present and you do not have
eyes to see, you will not be able to understand what is red,
white, yellow, or blue. If you wish to see, you must use your
eyes. The sounds are transmitted to your mind through
your ears, and the colors are transmitted to your mind
through the eyes. Likewise, spiritual things need to be
touched by the spirit.

If God wants to have fellowship and communion with
us, yet we do not have a heart, it is impossible for Him to
do so. Our heart is like the electric switch; when it is turned
on, the light goes on. When it is shut off, the light goes out.
If our heart is open to God, it is easy for God to have
fellowship with us, but if our heart is closed to God, it is
difficult for Him to have fellowship with us. It is true that
God's life is in us, but the heart is the switch of this life.
Whether God's life can pass through our spirit to the
conscience, whether His life can reach our mind through
the spirit, whether His life can reach our will through the
spirit or touch our emotion through the spirit, is a matter of
the heart. If the heart is open, God's life has a way; if the
heart is closed, God's life has no way.

The Heart can Hinder the Moving of Life

When the Holy Spirit regenerated us, we received the
uncreated life of God. This life is powerful and without
limitation. It is not restricted by space or time. But if our
heart has problems, God's life will be greatly hindered. If
there are problems with our conscience, our mind, our will,
or our emotions, God's life will be hindered. God's life has
been imparted into our spirit, but this life desires to spread
out and move into the different parts of our inward being.
If there is any part in us which has problems, this life will
be hindered and stopped.

Everyone who belongs to the Lord by God's grace has
God's life in him. This is definite and cannot be denied.

That God's life is alive and lives in us also cannot be denied. Because we have God's life in us, we receive revelation and enlightenment. His voice and feeling are within us. Why then do so many of God's children say, "I do not receive revelation or enlightenment, and I do not have His voice or feeling"? Does this mean that God's life in them is not real? Does it mean that God's life is not living? No, God's life is definitely real and definitely alive. Furthermore, God's life is living in them. The reason they do not receive revelation or enlightenment, the reason they do not hear His voice nor sense the feeling, is because on their part there is a heart problem. Perhaps there is a problem in the conscience. Some sin which the conscience is condemning may need to be dealt with. Or perhaps the mind has the problem of being full of anxieties, worries, evil thoughts, reasonings, or doubts. There may be a problem with the will, such as stubbornly holding on to our opinion or being unwilling to obey. The emotion also may be full of fleshly desires or natural inclinations. At any rate, there is some part in the heart which has a problem.

God's life has been imparted into us, and this life wants to move out from the spirit. But on our part we do not allow it to get through. Sometimes our conscience will not allow it through; sometimes our mind will not let it through; sometimes our will, and at other times our emotions, will not allow the life through. Therefore God's life cannot manifest itself through us. We must remember that when God's life moves through us it must pass through the different parts of our heart. If any part of the heart has problems, it will hinder the moving of God's life.

This can be proved by Ephesians 4:17-19: "This therefore I say and testify in the Lord, that you no longer walk as the nations also walk in the vanity of their mind, being darkened in their understanding, estranged from the life of God because of the ignorance which is in them, because of the hardness of their heart; who having ceased from feeling have given themselves over to lewdness to work all uncleanness in greedy unsatisfied lust." The word "mind" in verse 17 is *nous* in the Greek text. This word is used twenty-four times in the New Testament. Sometimes it is translated "mind" (as in Luke 24:45; Rom. 1:28; 7:23, 25; 11:34; 12:2; 14:5; 1 Cor. 1:10; 2:16; Eph. 4:17, 23; Col. 2:18; 2 Thes. 2:2; 1 Tim. 6:5; 2 Tim. 3:8; Titus 1:15; Rev. 17:9), and other times "understanding" (as in 1 Cor. 14:14-15, 19; Phil. 4:7; Rev. 13:18). The word *nous* in meaning includes both mind and understanding. In our human being there are three organs of perception: in our body there is the brain, in our spirit there is the intuition, and in our soul there is the mind. Our mind should be governed by our intuition. We all understand the matter of the brain in our body, but the intuition is hidden and less obvious. Sometimes we feel it and sometimes we do not; sometimes it urges us and sometimes it stops us. This we call the intuition. In between the intuition and the brain is our mind. The mind expresses the meaning of the intuition and causes the brain to make it clear. However, even if our intuition is strong and our brain is healthy, if the mind has a problem, the meaning within us cannot be made known. The *nous* in Ephesians 4:17 is an organ which is capable of thinking. It can be likened to our eyes. But the word "understanding" in verse 18, which in Greek is *dianoia,* defines the function of this organ and can be likened to our seeing. It is the power to understand.

Man's vain mind (the *nous*) is his imagination, his "castles in the air." This kind of mind is always filled with vain thoughts. On a certain occasion, after a preacher had finished his message, he asked some in the congregation to pray. In the course of one man's prayer, he said something about 250 strings of money. (In those days money was counted by strings.) The mind of this man was entirely filled with the imaginations of wealth. When God's life moved into this part of his being, how could it pass through? From this example, we see that whether it be a person, a matter, or a thing, it can all become an imagination to occupy our mind. Whenever our mind is occupied by some imagination, God's life is choked (Matt. 13:22).

When a man's mind is occupied by some imagination, his understanding becomes darkened and the power to understand becomes weakened. Once there was a young Christian who was occupied by a certain matter. He continued to turn the matter over and over in his mind until he was fully exhausted by it. At one moment he thought it was God's will; at another moment he thought it was not God's will. His mind was continually turning, with the result that he became confused. This means that his *dianoia*, his understanding, became darkened.

The reasons the mind becomes vain, the understanding darkens, and we become estranged from the life of God are due to our inner ignorance and the hardness of our heart which cause us to forsake all feeling. The heart may become hardened to such an extent that it no longer has any feeling. For this reason, the source of the problem is in the heart.

In summary, we can say that when the heart is hardened, we become estranged from the life of God, we become ignorant and unable to understand. The result is that the growth of life is hindered. Therefore, we must realize that it is not that the law of life does not move in us — the law of life is always waiting to spread out through our inward parts. However, if the different parts of our heart have problems, the moving of the life will be hindered. Thus, in order for the life of God to spread and move without hindrance, the heart must first have no problem.

The Softening of the Stony Heart and the Moving of Life

Ezekiel 36:25-27 speaks of at least five things: 1) we have been cleansed with clean water; 2) we have been given a new heart; 3) we have a new spirit within us; 4) our stony heart has been removed, and we have been given a heart of flesh; and 5) God's Spirit has been put within us. The result of putting these five things together is that we might walk in God's statutes and keep His ordinances. We have already pointed out that God has given us a new heart with a new spirit and that the Holy Spirit dwells within us. Now we shall give attention to the matter of how God removes our stony heart and gives us a heart of flesh. We must realize that when we speak of a stony heart and a fleshly heart, it does not mean that we have two hearts. We have only one heart. A stony heart refers to the hardness of the heart, while the fleshly heart refers to the softness of the heart; but the heart is still one. When we were saved, God gave us a fleshly heart, but our stony heart was still there. We could say that on one hand we had a fleshly heart, while on the other hand we had a stony heart. The removal of the stony heart is not something which occurs all at once, but is a gradual softening. To what extent God's life can grow in us depends completely upon how much our heart is softened. Our stony heart must be gradually transformed into a fleshly heart so that God's life can move out with no hindrance.

Among God's children, many have had the following experience: first they were saved and their hardened heart became softened, but not completely softened. At the time of their salvation their heart was softened perhaps seventy percent, but after a while their heart becomes hardened again. It seems as if they have gone back to their former condition. Moreover, this hardening of the heart seems worse than before. Perhaps the heart is caught by certain things, touched by a certain person, entangled by some object, or attracted by a certain job. These things begin to drag the man down. They are all problems of the heart. Whether the life can grow and spread in us depends completely upon whether our heart is transformed. It depends upon whether our heart is soft or hard. If our heart is caught by things other than God, whether it is some thing, some person, or some matter, it will always hinder the moving of life. Therefore, God wants to transform our heart. He will continue to transform us until our heart is completely changed into a fleshly heart. Then God's Spirit will cause the life in us to move out in a strong way.

When God's life desires to move out within us, He always touches our heart first, causing our stony heart to be softened. Some people are touched by God's love, others by His disciplining. When the children of Israel turned away from God, He smote them and they turned back to Him. Another example is that of a sister who was captured by her child, overly treasuring it. God spoke once, but she would not listen. God spoke twice and three times, but still she would not listen. Then God took the child away. At that time her heart was turned to God. Another brother was ensnared by his business. God spoke once, twice, five times, ten times, but he would not listen. Then God caused his business to fall apart. At that point he was turned to God. Some who have served God have been caught by the work — being busy from morning till night. It is true that the work is something spiritual, but it can capture the heart and take the place of God. To a certain one in such a situation God spoke once, but he would not listen. God spoke ten times, and still he would not listen. God struck him and he fell; his heart became enlightened, and thus he turned to God. Some brothers and sisters have their special practice, their special merit, or their special righteousness. But their practice, merit, or righteousness becomes their boast, the yardstick by which they measure others. These things crowd their heart. God speaks to them once, twice, ten times, twenty times — but they do not listen. Then God's hand comes upon them. At that time they become enlightened and prostrate themselves before God. Their hearts are completely turned to God. By such a work God is transforming a stony heart into a fleshly heart so that His life can move without any hindrance. If your heart has been touched by God, you will spontaneously say, "O God, I consecrate myself to You. I want You to turn my heart wholly toward You." When you offer yourself in such a way and allow God to do the work, He will move in you, and when He moves you will see something, hear something, and feel something. If you are willing to obey God, His life will move out into your conscience, into your mind, into your will, and into your emotions. In this manner, God's life will continue to move in you without ceasing.

Two Conditions for the Moving of Life

The law of life should be continually moving out. God wants to move out through the different inward parts of our being, but many times when the law of life moves it runs into a hard wall and cannot get through. There is a hindrance to the moving. Therefore, in order for the life to move and get through, we need to fulfill two conditions.

Obeying the First Sense of Life

The first condition is to obey the first sense of life. Unless a man is not regenerated, he will have some sense of life. A Christian who was a medical doctor asked a preacher the following question: "Both the beginning and the growth of our spiritual life start with hunger and thirst. However, many people do not feel hungry or thirsty. When that is the case, how can we cause them to become hungry and thirsty?" The reply was: "You are a medical doctor. You know that a man has life. Unless a man is dead, he will have some appetite. Then how do you increase his appetite? You prescribe something for him to increase his appetite. As he takes medicine, his appetite increases little by little. You continue this until his appetite is restored to normal. Therefore, whenever we have a little sense, we should obey this sense. When we obey this sense, our hunger and thirst increase slightly. When we obey more, the hunger and thirst increases again and our sense becomes stronger. Then we obey a little more. The more we obey, the stronger the sense will be. By taking this way we become alive from within." The Lord's life moves within us in the same way. It moves into our emotion, causing us to turn to God; it moves into our mind, causing us to turn to God; then it moves into our will, causing us to turn to God. By such continuous moving and turning, the life within us will be increased, deepened, and caused to grow. Therefore, we need to begin by obeying the least sense. Whenever there is a sense, we should obey.

Some will ask, "After obeying, what is next?" The answer is that before you obey the first sense you need not worry about the next step. According to the Scriptures, God never gives a man two senses at the same time. Abraham is an example. When he went out, he did not know where he was going (Heb. 11:8). He only knew that God wanted him to leave his home, his land, and his kindred and go into a place which God would show him (Acts 7:3). His first sense was to leave Ur of the Chaldees. The leading of life will never cause you to be independent, but always dependent. Abraham's experience was this: "I will take this first step. The next step I do not know." But as he walked step by step, he was fully dependent upon the Lord. God not only gave Abraham faith, but also wrought His life and nature into Abraham. Therefore, after obeying in the first step, you still need to continue to look to God, committing the second step to God through fellowship. By going on in this way, step by step, God will give you guidance.

When by God's grace we learn to follow Him from within, there will be feelings in us. When we go on in this way step by step and make a move which is beyond God, a move which does not match the life within us, we will immediately sense the forbidding of the Holy Spirit (Acts 16:6). This is very precious. Immediately, you will sense that the Spirit of Jesus suffers you not (Acts 16:7). If you obey the inner guidance again and again, either to do or to stop, you will grow in life. We repeat that we need to obey the first sense of life; even the least sense needs to be obeyed, for obeying is an important condition in allowing the life to move.

Loving God

Another condition is to love God. Mark 12:30 says, "Thou shalt love the Lord thy God with all thy heart, and with all thy soul, and with all thy mind, and with all thy strength." According to the original language, the word "mind" should be translated as "understanding" (*dianoia*). The verse shows that we have to use our whole heart, our whole soul, our whole understanding, and our whole strength to love God. God's Word shows us that loving God is related to the moving of life. The experience of many saints indicates that God first plants life into us, then touches our emotion with love. In the Gospel of John the emphasis is upon faith and also upon love. This gospel says that he who believes has eternal life (John 3:16). It also says, "If anyone loves Me, he will keep My word, and My Father will love him, and We will come to him and make an abode with him" (John 14:23). Faith means to receive the life into us, while love means to let the life flow out. Only faith can let the life come in, and only love can let the life flow out.

Therefore, we need to allow this love to reach our heart and flow into our emotion, mind, and will. We need to lift up our heads and say: "O my God, I want to love You with all my heart; I want to love You with all my soul; I want to love You with all my understanding; I want to love You with all my strength!" Anyone who truly does this will immediately see his mind change, his words change, and his behavior change. Everything within and without will be totally changed. For in this person a love story has taken place. Brothers and sisters, what God expects of us today is that our heart, our soul, our understanding, and our strength be touched by Him. Second Corinthians 3:16 says, "But whensoever it [the heart] shall turn to the Lord,

the veil is taken away." Whenever the heart turns to the
Lord, there will be the enlightenment, His voice, and the
sense of life.

So the question is not, What is enlightenment? What is
His voice? or What is the sense of life? the question is,
Where is your heart? If your heart is glued to some person,
matter, or thing; if it is attached to gifts, spiritual
experiences, or spiritual work, the spreading of life will be
hindered. The life within will be restrained from flowing
out, because it cannot pass through the heart. For this
reason, the heart must be turned to the Lord and fixed
upon God Himself. If our heart is turned to God, we will
have enlightenment within us, and we will hear His voice
and have the sense of life within. Brothers and sisters, if
we want to know God's will, we should not attempt to
understand with our mind; we should first turn our heart to
God. We must say: "O God, I desire only You; I want
nothing else." If we do this, we will very easily understand
God's will.

Romans 12:1-2 can prove these things for us. Paul first
said, "I beg you therefore, brothers, through the
compassions of God..." By these words he first touched
their emotion. Then he said, "Present your bodies a living
sacrifice." With these words his intention was to move the
will. Then he told them, "Be transformed by the renewing
of the mind, that you may prove by testing what the will of
God is, that which is good and well-pleasing and perfect."
This is the knowing of God's will in the mind. This shows
us that the life which is in man can spread to his emotion,
his will, and his mind. In this way the life permeates the
inward parts of our being and flows out through us. When
our heart is absolutely turned to God, He will impart
feeling within us, and He will guide and uphold us, so that
we may have the strength to obey Him. Then inwardly and
outwardly we shall be changed. Therefore, if we want the
life within us to spread to the outside, if we want the life to
grow, we need to love the Lord our God with all our heart,

with all our soul, with all our understanding, and with all our strength!

The Two Functions of the Moving of Life

God's life is continually moving. If we are willing to give Him the way by obeying Him, the life within will naturally grow and develop. If we allow this life to continue to move in us, letting it move into our conscience, our mind, our emotion, and our will, such continual moving will eliminate all the things we should not have and leave within us all the riches of God. In this way there is always something being eliminated and something being added. The more things are eliminated, the more things will be added. What is eliminated is something we should not have; what is added is something we should have. That which is eliminated is something of Adam, while that which is added is something of Christ. That which is eliminated is old, while that which is added is new. That which is eliminated is dead, while that which is added is living. By this process of gradual elimination and gradual addition, the life within us grows.

When God's life is thus moving within us, there are two functions. The first is death and the second is resurrection. The function of death is to remove the illness, while the function of resurrection is to give us health. The first element of the Lord's cross is death, while the second element is life. Romans 6 tells us that these two elements are the most powerful and useful elements in the life of Christ. The cross simply means that when our heart is touched by God we offer ourselves to Him so that His life can continue to move within us. When His life is moving, there is an element which puts us to death. This function of death will eliminate the things in us which we should not have. It will eliminate the things which are contrary to God, contrary to life, and contrary to the Holy Spirit. On the other hand, there is an element of life which makes us alive. This function of life causes us to live out all the riches of the Godhead, so that we are full of light, full of joy, and full of peace. The death of Christ and the life of Christ thus cause us to be delivered from sin and from all that God hates and condemns. On the other hand, they cause us to receive something fresh, something illuminating, something of joy and peace. Just as there is the elimination, there is also the addition. We need to allow God's life to operate, to move in us. Whenever His life is moving, something is being eliminated and something is being added. Every time God's life moves in us we die a little more, and at the same time we live a little more. The more God's life moves and eliminates the things which should not be there, the more the things which should be there will be added; the more the death is eliminated, the more the life will be increased. May we go on according to the moving of God's life so that His life in us can reach all the different parts, moving without hindrance, always eliminating something and always adding something.

The Great Power of the Moving of Life

Hebrews 8:7 says, "For if that first covenant was faultless, no place would have been sought for a second." We have mentioned before that the reason the first covenant had fault was not because the covenant itself was faulty, but because it was weak when applied to man. The first covenant composed of the commandments of letters was written upon stone tablets. It could only demand man to keep the law; it could not give man the power to do it. The reason the new covenant is a better covenant is because through it the law is imparted into man; it is inscribed on man's heart. The new covenant law of life can cause man to obey God's will and does not need man's teaching. It enables man to know God from within. Therefore, we say that the new covenant is exceedingly glorious and extremely precious.

In the new covenant God's laws are put into the inward parts of man. If God's life moves to a certain part and cannot get through, it is hindered and will remain stopped there. It will be unable to spread out. This does not mean that there is something which the new covenant cannot do. No, the new covenant can do all things, for the new covenant means that "with God all things are possible." The reason the new covenant can do all things is because the moving of this life is powerful. This power is the power of the indestructible life (Heb. 7:16). The mighty power of the moving of this life is the same power which raised the Lord Jesus from the dead (Eph. 1:20). It is also the power of the moving of this life which is able to do superabundantly above all that we ask or think (Eph. 3:20).

Let us now consider some examples.

It Can Cause Man's Heart to Turn to God

We are told in 2 Corinthians 3:14-16 that the hearts of the children of Israel became hardened. When they read the Old Testament, there was a veil on their hearts. It also tells us that whenever their hearts would turn to the Lord, the veil would be taken away. This makes it clear that the veil of the Israelites was their hard heart, a heart which did not want the Lord. Whenever their hearts would turn to the Lord, the veil would be taken away. Therefore, whenever we have a veil within us, it means that our heart has a problem.

The question then is how can our heart be turned to the Lord? The Scripture says that man's "heart is in the hand of Jehovah as the watercourses: He turneth it whithersoever He will" (Prov. 21:1). As long as we are willing to put our heart in God's hand He can turn us.

If we are willing to pray to the Lord saying, "Lord, I pray that You will turn my heart unto Your testimonies, and not to covetousness" (Psa. 119:36), God will be able to turn our heart. If we are those who are truly saved, whose heart has been renewed, even if we have turned to other things and become cold, yet we clearly realize within us that God is having mercy toward us, His life keeps moving within us, until one day it will move us to say aloud or in silence, "O God, I pray that You will turn my heart." Based on this slight giving in, the life will move further and increase more. In this way our heart is stirred up and is being turned to the Lord.

It Enables Man to Obey God

Philippians 2:12-13 says, "Even as you have always obeyed, not only as in my presence, but now much rather in my absence, work out your own salvation with fear and trembling." How could they do this? The answer follows: "For it is God Who operates in you both the willing and the working for His good pleasure." Many times, not only are we not able to obey God, but we do not want to obey God. However, if we are truly saved and our heart has been touched, even though at times we backslide and our heart becomes hardened, yet within us we know the story: God has mercy toward us, His life is still moving in us, and eventually it will move until our heart will again have the desire to obey God. We will then decide to obey God, and we will also be enabled to obey God. The reason is simply that God's life has moved into our emotion and will. It has moved to the extent that we become able to obey God.

The conscience of a certain sister was so accused that she felt she would never want God's will and never be able to obey God again. It seemed that all she waited for was the verdict of God's judgment, so great was her suffering. But at this same time there was a prayer within her. She whispered to God: "O God, I may not be able to seek Your will, but I still ask You to make me to seek Your will. Even though I cannot obey You, I still ask You to cause me to obey You." That was a wonderful prayer. Philippians 2:13 upheld her that day. She realized that if God had not been working in her heart she would not have had such a prayer. Since God's moving had caused her to pray such a prayer, God must also be able to cause her to obey His will, for His moving is for the accomplishment of His good pleasure. When she saw this, she was revived with joy.

It Enables Man to Do the Works Which God Has Prepared

Ephesians 2:10 says, "We are His workmanship, created in Christ Jesus for good works, which God before prepared that we should walk in them." This work was accomplished by God Himself in Christ Jesus. We can say that it is God's masterpiece. A masterpiece is simply the most excellent, fine piece of work, the best production. Nothing can be better than a masterpiece. God has not only saved His people, but in Christ Jesus He has made them into a masterpiece. This has been done through the working of the power of His life in man. This is an aspect of the characteristic of the new covenant. God has made man into such a masterpiece that He could not do better. This has not been done so that man could be satisfied in himself, but so that God's purpose of fulfilling the good works which He has prepared before might be accomplished. What a wonderfully high standard! The good works which God has prepared for us must be something which He considers to be good. Only that which has its origin in love is the good works which God considers good (Matt. 19:17). Any good work that does not originate from love, even bestowing all our goods to feed the poor, or even giving our body to be burned for others, is still not profitable (1 Cor. 13:3). The good works which originate from love are not ordinary good works, but good works which issue from a life of love and which are done based on the principle of love. The good works which God has prepared for us to do can only be fulfilled and lived out by God's life. Praise God, He has saved us and put His life in us! It is through the power of this life that the masterpiece can be accomplished and that we can do the good works which He has prepared for us. This is the gospel. This is the glory of the new covenant! Hallelujah!

It Enables Man to Labor and Strive

The Apostle Paul said: "His grace which was bestowed upon me was not found vain" (1 Cor. 15:10). We know this was true because he labored more abundantly than all the other apostles. Yet he says, "Not I, but the grace of God which was with me." He could labor more abundantly than others, not because his body was stronger, nor because he was more diligent than others, but because the grace of God was with him. He says further, "Whom we announce, warning every man and teaching every man in all wisdom, that we may present every man full grown in Christ; for which also I labor, struggling according to His operation which operates in me in power" (Col. 1:28-29). The word "power" in verse 29 can also be translated "exploding power." In other words, what God was operating inwardly was an exploding power; hence, what Paul was working outwardly was also an exploding power. The Apostle Paul worked, not because he was energetic in himself, but because within him there was an exploding power. This exploding power exploded continually within him, enabling him to labor diligently and to struggle to bring all men before God perfect in Christ. This exploding power is the power of the working of God's life! It is the power of this life which enables us to labor diligently and to strive in our work.

To labor more abundantly and to strive or struggle prove both the inner grace and the power of the inner life. This indicates that God gives us grace, not to make us those who appreciate spirituality, nor that we might enjoy our own spirituality, but that we may be more diligent laboring and striving more than others. If anyone says that he is the Lord's servant, and yet continues to love himself, to be lazy, and not to work, then he is not only slothful, he is also surely evil (Matt. 25:26). This kind of servant is condemned by the Lord. Therefore, we must not talk about empty doctrines. We must look to God that we may live out His grace and manifest His power.

It Enables Man to Have a Living and Fresh Service

Before considering how this life enables us to have a living and fresh service, let us read three passages. The first is 2 Corinthians 3:5-6: "Not that we are sufficient of ourselves, to account anything as from ourselves; but our sufficiency is from God; who also made us sufficient as ministers of a new covenant; not of the letter, but of the spirit: for the letter killeth, but the spirit giveth life."

The second is Romans 7:6: "But now we are discharged from the law, having died to that in which we were held, that we should serve as slaves in newness of spirit and not in oldness of letter."

The third passage is Romans 2:28-29: "For he is not a Jew who is one outwardly; neither the circumcision which is outward in the flesh: but he is a Jew who is one inwardly; and circumcision is of the heart, in the spirit, not in the letter, whose praise is not from men, but from God."

These three passages of Scripture show that there is a great difference between the service of the new covenant and that of the old. Service in the old covenant was of the letter, but service in the new covenant is of the spirit. The service of the old covenant was old, but the service of the new covenant is fresh. The service of the old covenant killed, but the service of the new covenant gives life. In other words, the service in the old covenant was according to the written letter, commandment after commandment. It was a service according to form. But the service in the new covenant is according to the Spirit. In the new covenant the Spirit dictates how man should act, and he acts accordingly; the Spirit dictates how man should speak, and he speaks accordingly; the Spirit tells man how to pray, and he prays in that way.

We may say that the service of the old covenant was outward, while the service of the new covenant is inward. The service of "the letter" in the old covenant resulted only in death, while the service of "the spirit" in the new covenant results in giving man life. In other words, the service which is by "the letter" is dead, while the service which is by "the letter" is old, but service which is based on living "in Christ" is alive. Service which is according to "the letter" is old, but service which is the result of living "in Christ" is fresh. Service which is according to "the letter" is only in letters, but service which comes from living "in Christ" is spiritual.

We can say then that any kind of service which is outward, according to the letter, and in oldness, is the service of the old covenant. But any service which is inward, according to the spirit, and in newness, is the service of the new covenant. Any service which comes from copying or imitating something outward is not the service of the new covenant. The service of the new covenant is something which is the result of having a relationship with Christ and is worked out from within. The service of the new covenant is spiritual, of revelation, and in newness. The service of the new covenant is of God, through God, and to God (Rom. 11:36). The strength of service is of Him, the course of service is through Him, and the result of service is unto Him. This is spiritual service. This is living service, and this is the new covenant service.

Paul says, "Not that we are sufficient of ourselves, to account anything as from ourselves; but our sufficiency is from God; who also made us sufficient as ministers of a new covenant" (2 Cor. 3:5-6). God was working in them to such an extent that they were enabled to become ministers of the new covenant, that is, they became the serving ones under the new covenant. Paul also said, "Of which I became a minister according to the gift of the grace of God, which was given to me according to the operation of His power" (Eph. 3:7). Paul said clearly that his becoming a minister of the gospel was according to the gift of God's grace. This gift was not tongues, nor was it visions, miracles, wonders, healing, or casting out of demons — although Paul had all of these gifts (see 1 Cor. 14:18; Acts 13:9-11; 14:8-10; 16:9, 16-18; 18:9). Neither was this gift excellency of speech or of wisdom (1 Cor. 2:1). This gift was not something which came down suddenly out of heaven. Paul says very clearly that this gift was given to him according to the operation of God's power. It was not a miraculous gift, but a gift of grace. It came through the power of God's operation in Paul. This gift enabled Paul to "preach to the nations the unsearchable riches of Christ as the gospel, and to bring to light what is the dispensation of the mystery, which from the ages has been hidden in God, Who created all things" (Eph. 3:8-9). This gift is marvelous! This marvelous gift was given to him according to the power of God's operation.

Christ Being Formed in Us, Transformation, and Conformity to Him

When the law of life is allowed to move in us without hindrance, it will develop to a state where Christ can be formed in us (Gal. 4:19). When Christ is gradually formed in us, we will be transformed (2 Cor. 3:18). The goal of transformation is to be like Him (1 John 3:2). Christ being formed in us cannot be separated from the working of God's life in us. To the extent that God's life becomes mingled with us, Christ will be formed in us, and to that extent we will be transformed.

To the extent that a man is filled with the life of Christ, lives Christ out, and expresses Christ, he is conformed to the image of God's Son, as mentioned in Romans 8:29. This is what Paul pursued, and this was Paul's experience (see Phil 3:10; 1:20). This can also be our experience today and should be the pursuit of every child of God. As far as being fully like Him is concerned, we must wait until the Lord appears (1 John 3:2). That day will be the time of the redemption of our body (Eph. 1:14; 4:30; Rom. 8:23). At that time we will be completely like Him.

Christ Being Formed in Us

A simple illustration will help us to see what it means to

have Christ formed in us. In an egg there is the life of a chicken. However, if during the first days of incubation you use a light to look through the egg, you cannot tell which part is the head and which is the foot. It is when the chicken is almost ready to break through the shell and come out that you can see what the complete shape of the chicken is. At that time we can say that the chicken has been formed inside the egg. In like manner, Christ's life in immature Christians is not well-formed. It is only formed in grown-up Christians. The life of Christ is complete, but it is restricted by us. Therefore, Christ is not yet fully formed in us. This means that the growth of life is hindered.

Paul was in travail again for the Galatian believers until Christ was formed in them (Gal. 4:19). We see from this that the formation of Christ is very important. Paul was not speaking empty words here, nor was he feeling sorry for himself. He was travailing again, which takes time, love, intercession, tears, and daily expectation. How many of God's children today have Christ formed in them? How many who serve the Lord care for the spiritual state of God's children and labor painfully in spiritual birth? Oh, when we speak of this we repent, we are pained, and we weep, not only because we are in such a poor situation, but that even towards some of God's children our love is so inadequate.

Some children of God are immature and abnormal. Others even shrink back and fall. Can we put all the blame on them for their poor situation? Can we feel at ease and go on day after day without feeling sorrow and praying for them? "O God, forgive us and be merciful to us. Give us time to learn and to experience. Give us time to travail again for those who are like the Galatian believers."

Transformation

According to Romans 12:1-2 there are two prerequisites for transformation: one is the presentation of our bodies;

the other is the renewing of our mind. The presentation of our body can be likened to regeneration — it is done once for all; whereas transformation is a process and is something gradual.

Let us now consider specifically the relationship between the mind and transformation. Romans 12:2 says, "Be transformed by the renewing of the mind." Ephesians 4:23 says, "And are renewed in the spirit of your mind." Both of these verses refer to the relationship between the renewing of the mind and transformation. The work of the Holy Spirit is always from the center to the circumference. Because the spirit is especially related to the mind, the spirit must be renewed first; then the mind must be renewed; finally, man's behavior will gradually be changed.

Repentance means to have a change of mind; it means that the eyes have been opened. To have our mind renewed simply means that our eyes have been enlightened. The more our mind is renewed, the more we are transformed. Day by day, through the light of life, God is causing us to know ourselves, to repudiate ourselves, to know the reality of the inner life, and to experience putting off the old man and putting on the new man regarding our manner of life. This is a matter of our subjective experience. Objectively speaking, Christians have already put off, as regards their former manner of life, the old man, and have also put on the new man (Eph. 4:22, 24; Col. 3:10). These are all facts which have been accomplished in Christ.

We must realize that transformation is not like regeneration. Regeneration is something that happens once for all, but transformation is a daily gradual process. We must ask ourselves this question: to what extent have I experienced transformation? If there has been no change in us since the time we became a Christian, if we are still self-loving, self-pitying, selfish, proud, self-exalting, and full of worry and doubt, then it is questionable whether we have really met the light. If, as we go on, we become more cold, more hardened, more proud, more conceited, more loose and unruly, then there is illness either in our heart or in our mind. If this is the case, we need to humble ourselves and begin again to deal with our heart. We need to ask the Lord to be merciful to us, to enlighten us and to give us strength to get rid of any sin and every bit of self that is hindering the move of the law of life.

The Holy Spirit says, "Today if you hear His voice, do not harden your hearts . . ." (Heb. 3:7-8). May the Lord be merciful to us that our heart may be softened before Him. At the same time we need to believe Philippians 2:13: "For it is God Who operates in you both the willing and the working for His good pleasure." This is the characteristic of the new covenant. This is also the glory of the new covenant. We must praise God!

Transformation and Conformation

Conformation spoken of in Romans 8:29 and Philippians 3:10 means in the original text to be of like form and nature or to be alike. This Greek word is used only three times in the New Testament: in Romans 8:29, in Philippians 3:21, where it is used as an adjective, and in Philippians 3:10, where it is used as a verb.

What is the difference in being transformed and being conformed? Transformation speaks of a process, while conformation speaks of the completed work. Transformation means that the Lord's life gradually grows up in us, that we are the same as the Lord. Conformation means that we are transformed completely and are the same in form and nature as the Lord. To be conformed can be compared to something which comes out of a mold. When a smith puts melted brass into a mold, his melted brass takes the shape of the mold. It could also be likened to a person making a cake who puts the dough into a mold. The result is that the cake becomes the same in shape as the mold. Our likeness to the Lord will be a likeness to this degree.

Romans 8:29 says, ". . . to be conformed to the image of

His Son." This means that our image will be the same as that of the Lord's glorified humanity. If a person wants to be transformed and be conformed to the image of the prototype that God has ordained, he must have a change of nature from within. God's life must enter into his spirit and permeate his whole being until he is completely changed in nature. Accordingly, there will be a complete conformation in image. Thus the Spirit of the Lord works step by step, from glory to glory (2 Cor. 3:17-18). Praise the Lord for such a work!

Here again we need to consider the matter of the heart. Second Corinthians 3:18 says, "We all, with unveiled face beholding as a mirror the glory of the Lord, are being transformed into the same image from glory to glory, even as from the Lord the Spirit" (lit.). Here a mirror is used as an illustration. A mirror can only reflect what it is directed at, what is in front of it. Likewise in our daily life, the more we see Christ, the more we will reflect Christ. An unveiled face means that our face is not covered with a veil; thus we can see Christ in a complete way. If we have a veil over our face, either we will not see Christ at all or we will see Him in an incomplete way. When 2 Corinthians 3:12-16 is examined carefully, it is apparent that the veil was due to the fact that the heart did not want the Lord. In the past, Moses' face shone because God spoke to him. Because the Israelites feared the light of the shining of his face, they hesitated to draw near to him. Therefore, when Moses came into the presence of God he removed the veil, but when he came out he used the veil to cover his face again (Exo. 34:29-35). The veil upon Moses' face speaks of the condition of the children of Israel, that their hearts were far from God. Later, the Israelites were again in the same condition of being afraid of the light. They did not want the light. The veil upon their heart had not yet been removed: therefore, when they read the Old Testament they could not understand it. Verse 16 says very clearly that whenever their heart turned to the Lord the veil was taken away. This is the key to whether or not we can clearly see the Lord. If our heart is turned to other things, it will be as if it were covered with a veil, and naturally our life will be as if under a dim light and will reflect Christ in an incomplete way.

It is a problem of the heart, a problem of the mirror. Whenever we feel that there is a barrier, a veil, between the Lord and us, our heart needs to be turned once again to the Lord. When our heart is turned to the Lord we can see clearly, and the reflection is also clear.

To be Like Him

We have said already that the goal of transformation is to be like Him. But complete likeness to Him must wait until the Lord appears. That is the time of the redemption of our body. Then we will be wholly like Him. For this reason we must also say a word concerning the redemption of the body. We have seen that when Adam fell the spirit died first, and man became completely controlled by the soul and completely in the flesh. Later, the body also died (Gen. 5:5; Rom. 8:11). This means that the death which took place in the spirit eventually reached the body.

When man is regenerated his spirit is made alive first. Then through the work of the cross the Holy Spirit puts to death the evil practices of our body (Rom. 8:13; Col. 3:5), causing us to deny ourselves daily (Luke 9:23). Furthermore, through the operation of the life in us day by day we are being changed increasingly both in our nature and in our form, so that we may be conformed to the image of the Son of God. Eventually one day when the Lord appears "we shall be like him; for we shall see him even as he is" (1 John 3:2). This is the redemption of the body for which Paul was waiting (Rom. 8:23). This matter is also mentioned in Philippians 3:21, where Paul says that the Lord Jesus will "transfigure the body of our humiliation, conforming it to the body of His glory, according to the operation of Him Who is able even to subject all things to Himself."

From these verses we see that God's salvation begins with making our spirit alive and ends with the redemption of our body. The phrase "you will live" mentioned in Romans 8:13 refers to our daily experience of living in the body. It does not refer to the redemption of our body. The Scriptures tell us that resurrection and transformation are a mystery (1 Cor. 15:51-52). The redemption of the body in which we are made like unto His own glorious body is also exceedingly glorious. The Apostle John believed that this would be fulfilled one day. Therefore, he said that when the Lord appears, we shall be like Him for we shall see Him as He is. This is the characteristic of the new covenant. This is also the glory of the new covenant! Brothers and sisters, let us not be too late in believing.

Purifying Oneself

Although the redemption of the body is clearly a matter of God's grace, nevertheless, after the Apostle John said that we should be like Him and see Him as He is, he immediately followed by saying: "And every one that hath this hope set on him purifieth himself, even as he is pure" (1 John 3:3).

Put into its context, this hope refers to the words "be like him." Purifying in this verse is different from being clean. To be clean means to be without defilement, but purifying means not only to be without defilement, but also to be without mixture. The way to purify ourselves is through the shining of the light of life within us (John 1:4), so that we may know ourselves (Psa. 36:9) and eliminate all that displeases Him.

We are those who have God's nature; therefore, according to the consciousness which comes from the nature of the life of God, we should deal not only with sin, but with all that is of ourselves and all that is not of God's will. This is the meaning of purifying ourselves. But there is a purification even deeper than this. A brother who has become learned in the Lord spoke of purification in this way: "The danger of spirituality is to experience victory and sanctification, to be fruitful in our work, to possess spiritual gifts and righteousnesses that are of life.... Deeper purification means that even that which comes from God's revelation, which issues from the resurrection life of Christ, should not be allowed to remain. There is the process of metabolism in the growth of life. ... this means that anything which comes from the resurrection life will never be lost; it will forever be fresh. However, it must be kept in the newness of the Holy Spirit and not merely remembered in the mind. That which has its source in His resurrection life will not be lost but will remain in us forever; it will become part of our life and be constituted into our being. Whenever that particular thing is required, we need only to take it in the Holy Spirit. Then it will be as fresh and living as if we had just seen it."

These words are not easily understood, but they do call forth a response in us. Brothers and sisters, if we have such a hope in Him, we will say to ourselves what the Apostle John said, "Everyone that hath this hope set on him purifieth himself"; and then we will rise up and walk according to the shining of the Holy Spirit.

God Desires to be God in the Law of Life

The continual moving of God's life in us has a great purpose. In the second part of Hebrews 8:10 it says, "I will be God to them, and they shall be a people to Me." This tells us what is on God's heart and what His purpose is from eternity to eternity. God wants to be our God, and we need to be His people according to the law of life. This is real and very wonderful. We shall now see from the Scriptures what an important matter in the universe this is.

God's Eternal Purpose

What does God intend to have in the universe? In Genesis 2 we see that after God had created man, He indicated that man should exercise his free will to choose His life. However, we are not told what God intended to have in the universe. Genesis 3 speaks of man's fall, but it does not tell us what the Devil was really after. It was not until God led the Israelites out of Egypt and brought them to Mount Sinai, where He declared the Ten Commandments, that He revealed what was on His heart. It was not until the Lord Jesus was tempted in the wilderness that He revealed what the Devil was really after, and it was not until the Lord prayed the prayer which He taught His disciples, that again He clearly spoke of God's true desire.

The first of the Ten Commandments is: "Thou shalt have no other gods before me." The second is: "Thou shalt not make unto thee a graven image, nor any likeness of any thing that is in heaven above, or that is in the earth beneath, or that is in the water under the earth: thou shalt not bow down thyself unto them, nor serve them: for I Jehovah thy God am a jealous God." The third commandment is: "Thou shalt not take the name of Jehovah thy God in vain." The fourth is: "Remember the sabbath day, to keep it holy" (Exo. 20:3-8).

In these four commandments God revealed His will and clearly unveiled His formal requirements for man. Here He spoke clearly of the purpose of His creation and the purpose of His redemption. The purpose is simply that God wants to be God. God is God, and He wants to be God among men.

In the New Testament there is a great revelation which parallels God's revelation upon Mount Sinai. It is the Lord's temptation in the wilderness. In the books of Ezekiel and Isaiah we are clearly told of the cherub which God had made, who later exalted himself to become equal with God. He rebelled against God, was judged by God (Ezek. 28:8, 12-19; Isa. 14:12-15), and became the Devil.

However, this matter was not as clearly revealed as it is in the Gospels when the Devil made his open bid to usurp God's position. The strongest part of the Devil's temptation of the Lord was: "... if You will fall down and worship me." But the Lord without any hesitation rebuked him saying, "Go, Satan." Then the Lord solemnly declared: "You shall worship the Lord your God, and Him only shall you serve" (Matt. 4:9-10). Oh, only God is God!

In the New Testament, the prayer which the Lord taught His disciples was also a great revelation. In this prayer, He also reveals God's will — that God wants to be God. The Lord said, "Pray, then, like this: Our Father Who is in the heavens, let Your name be sanctified" (Matt. 6:9). In the heavens God's name can only be used by God, but on earth there are people who take His name in vain, and yet He hides Himself as if He did not exist. However, one day our Lord taught His disciples to pray, "Our Father Who is in the heavens, let Your name be sanctified." The Lord's purpose in wanting us to pray in this way is that we would declare that only He is God. The rest are not. We need to glory in His holy name as the Psalmist did (Psa. 105:3). We need to say: "O Jehovah, our Lord, how excellent is thy name in all the earth" (Psa. 8:1). O God, may Your praise be perfected in "the mouth of babes and sucklings"! (Matt. 21:16).

God Desires to Dwell Among the Children of Israel as Their God

Although God is God, the marvelous fact is that He desires to dwell among men. God commanded Moses to build Him a sanctuary, saying clearly, "... that I may dwell among them" (Exo. 25:8). Again He said, "And I will dwell among the children of Israel, and will be their God. And they shall know that I am Jehovah their God, that brought them forth out of the land of Egypt, that I might dwell among them: I am Jehovah their God (Exo. 29:45-46). God wanted Moses to tell the children of Israel plainly that

He was Jehovah their God who brought them forth out of the land of Egypt to give them the land of Canaan and to be their God (Lev. 25:38). Leviticus 26:12 is clearer still: "And I will walk among you, and will be your God, and ye shall be my people." God is God! He is very high and very great! Yet He comes to dwell among men to be their God.

The Word Became Flesh, Dwelling Among Men, to Declare God

When the Word became flesh and tabernacled among us (John 1:14), this Word of life which was from the beginning was heard and seen and touched by man (1 John 1:1). "No one has ever seen God"; but now "the only begotten Son, Who is in the bosom of the Father, He has declared Him" (John 1:18). This is Emmanuel, God with us (Matt. 1:23).

God Dwells in the Church as God

When the church was built as a spiritual house (1 Pet. 2:5), it became God's dwelling place in spirit (Eph. 2:22). This is a very mysterious and glorious matter. When the Word became flesh and tabernacled among men, He was limited by space and time; but when God dwells in the church in spirit, He is limited by neither time nor space. Hallelujah!

In the Kingdom Age God Will be the God of the House of Israel

Although in the old covenant time the people of Israel forsook God, in the future God will make a new covenant with them. In the future He will impart His laws into their minds and inscribe them upon their hearts so that He may be their God (Heb. 8:10).

In Eternity Future God Will Dwell Among Men as God

One day the tabernacle of God will be with men: "And He shall tabernacle with them, and they shall be His peoples, and God Himself shall be with them" (Rev. 21:3).

This is most wonderful! "And He shall wipe away every tear from their eyes; and death shall be no more; nor sorrow, nor crying, nor pain — they shall be no more; for the former things have passed away" (Rev. 21:4). At that time God and man, man and God, will never be separated again. Hallelujah!

God as the Father and God as God

On the resurrection day Jesus told Mary Magdalene: "Go to My brothers and say to them, I ascend to My Father and your Father, and My God and your God" (John 20:17). This verse tells us that we have not only a Father but also a God. The difference between God as Father and God as God as shown in the Scripture is that God as the Father indicates His relation to individuals, while God as God indicates His relation to the whole universe. God as our Father is a matter of life, showing that we are related to Him as a son is related to a father; while God as God is a matter of position, showing that He is the Creator.

When we know God as the Father, we will dare to throw ourselves upon His bosom. And when we know God as God, we must bow down and worship Him. We are God's children, living in His love and gladly enjoying all that He gives us. We are also His people, standing upon the position of a man, worshipping and praising Him. Because God is God we need to worship Him in holy array (Psa. 29:2) and in fear (Psa. 5:7). Anyone who knows God as God in all things cannot but fear Him and pay attention to such things as his clothing and behavior. Anyone who is loose, careless, haughty, doing whatever he will, and allowing sin to remain, is one who does not know God as God.

We know that "there is no creature that is not manifest before Him, but all things are naked and laid bare to the eyes of Him to Whom we are accountable" (Heb. 4:13). Therefore, "Do not participate in the unfruitful works of darkness, but rather even expose them; for the things which are done by them in secret it is shameful even to speak of" (Eph. 5:11-12).

If a man is afraid to open up anything to God, that is called darkness. Anything which a man dares not open to God is a shame. Paul said, "Knowing therefore the fear of the Lord, we persuade men" (2 Cor. 5:11). We dare not but fear the Lord and entreat men, telling them that unless they are non-repentant or unsaved they must know that "our God is a consuming fire" (Heb. 12:29). If man does not deal seriously with all the sins which should be dealt with, he will fall, one day, into the hands of the living God. This will be a terrible experience (Heb. 10:31).

Do you think that God is sleeping because He temporarily hides Himself? God is patient and tolerant, waiting for you to repent. Do you think that He can be mocked? The Scriptures tell us "God is not mocked" (Gal. 6:7). Brothers and sisters, we must fear God.

If you know that God is God, you will want to be a man. The fall infected us with the desire to be God, but salvation once again instills in us the willing desire to be man. The principle of the Garden of Eden is that after eating the fruit of the tree of the knowledge of good and evil we will be like God (Gen. 3:5), but the principle of Golgotha is the restoration of our position as man. Thus, if we know God as God, we will stand in our position as man. Our Lord was born as a man in the house of a carpenter (Matt. 13:55). As a man He submitted Himself to the baptism of John the Baptist (Matt. 3:13-16). Three times as a man He rejected the temptation of the Devil (Matt. 4:1-10). Also as a man He suffered and was tried (Heb. 2:18). As a man He was mocked upon the cross and did not come down (Matt. 27:42-44). If the Lord took His position as a man, what about us?

The twenty-four elders of Revelation 4:4 are the elders of the whole universe. (The twenty-four elders already have the crowns, are already sitting upon the thrones, and have the number "twenty-four," which is not the number of the church; therefore, they must be the elders of the whole universe, representing the angels whom God created and being the elders among the angels.) Because they know God as the God of creation, they worship Him and say: "You are worthy, our Lord and God, to receive the glory and the honor and the power, for You have created all things, and because of Your will they were and have been created" (Rev. 4:11). When eventually they come to the wedding feast of the Lamb, they will still bow down and worship God, who sits upon the throne (Rev. 19:4).

When the angel flew in the air, preaching the eternal gospel to the people upon the earth, he said, "Fear God and give Him glory, because the hour of His judgment has come; and worship Him Who has made the heaven and the earth and the sea and springs of waters" (Rev. 14:6-7). This indicates that when we know God as God and the Creator we will worship Him.

Anyone who knows God as God and takes the position of a slave will worship Him (Rev. 22:9). Surely he who "sitteth in the temple of God, setting himself forth as God," is the one who opposes the Lord (2 Thes. 2:4). He who is able to do signs and deceive people upon the earth, telling them to worship the beast (Rev. 13:14-15) is surely the false Christ (Matt. 24:23-24). Anyone who knows God as God will worship Him. This is what glorifies God.

God as God in the Law of Life

Now we must see that God has imparted His law into our mind and inscribed it upon our heart for the purpose that He may be our God in the law of life and that we may be His people in the law of life. The second half of Hebrews 8:10 immediately follows what has gone before. It does not say here that God wants to be our God upon the throne. Rather it says that God wants to be our God in the law of life and that He wants us to be His people in the law of life. We and God, God and we, both have our relationships in the law of life. If we are not in the law of life, we cannot touch God. If we live in the law of life, we shall be God's people and God will be our God. The only way to draw near to Him, serve Him, and worship Him is by touching God in the law of life.

Why is it that God becomes our God and we become His people in the law of life? To explain this we need once again to consider man's creation and new birth. Because God is Spirit, anyone who desires to have fellowship with Him must have a spirit. When God made Adam, there was an element in him which was the same as God's. That element in man was the spirit. When Adam fell and became alienated from God's life, his spirit was dead to God. However, due to God's redemption, when man repents and believes, not only does his spirit become alive, but he also receives God's uncreated life. Through the Holy Spirit, God enters into us and dwells in us, and from that point on we can worship God in spirit and in reality. John 4:23-24 is very clear. Verse 24 says that "God is Spirit; and those who worship Him must worship in spirit and reality." This means that only the element in man which is the same as God can worship God. Only the spirit can worship Spirit. Only worship which is in the spirit is true worship. This kind of worship is not something in which one uses his mind; neither is it something in which one uses his emotions or will. This worship is in spirit and in reality. Verse 23 says, "The true worshippers shall worship the Father in spirit and reality; for the Father seeks such to worship Him." This is very meaningful. When we read this with what follows, we see that if a man desires to worship God, he must first know how to worship the Father. If a person does not have the relationship of Father and son with God, he does not yet have life and his spirit is still dead; he cannot worship God. When a person is born again, his spirit is made alive, he becomes a child of God, and he can have fellowship with God. It is such that the Father wants to worship Him. Therefore, before we can be God's people, we must first become God's children. For this reason we say that God becomes our God in the law of life, and we are God's people in the law of life.

Titus 2:14 says, "Who gave Himself for us, that He might redeem us from all lawlessness and purify to Himself a people for His own possession, zealous of good works." As God's peculiar people we become His acquired possession (Eph. 1:14). The reason we can become God's peculiar people is because He is our God in the law of life, and we are His people in the law of life.

Revelation 21:7 says, "He who overcomes shall inherit these things, and I will be God to him, and he shall be a son to Me." In eternity, as far as the relationship of life and the individual relationship are concerned, we will be sons to God; but as far as God's position and our knowledge of Him as God are concerned, He shall be our God. How glorious this is!

Finally, we must speak to ourselves the same words that were spoken to the Apostle John: "Worship God" (Rev. 22:9).

CHAPTER EIGHT

THE CHARACTERISTICS OF THE CONTENT OF THE NEW COVENANT

III. INWARD KNOWLEDGE

Regarding the characteristics of the content of the new covenant, we have already mentioned two main aspects. It is true that God is propitious to our unrighteousnesses and no longer remembers our sins. This is the grace of God given to us in the new covenant. But this is merely a procedure by which God achieves His eternal purpose. It is also true that God becomes our God and we become His people in the law of life. The new covenant, however, does not stop there, but continues with, "They shall by no means teach each one his fellow citizen and each one his brother, saying, Know the Lord, for all shall know Me from the little one to the great among them" (Heb. 8:11). This is the deeper knowledge of God. This is knowing God Himself. Through the Spirit, God is bringing His redeemed ones to the highest point, that is, to know Himself. God imparts His laws into our mind and inscribes them upon our hearts. This is merely a procedure by which God achieves His deeper purpose, which is to know God Himself. While it is true that to have fellowship with God is purposeful in itself, at the same time the fellowship we have with God is His procedure to obtain a deeper purpose, which is to know God Himself. We know that God's purpose is to constitute us with Himself that He may become completely blended with us. Thus the characteristic of the new covenant is that man may know God Himself in the law of life, and in this way fulfill God's purpose.

Hosea 4:6 says, "My people are destroyed for lack of knowledge." The lack of knowledge in this verse is the lack of knowing God Himself. The children of Israel were disobedient to the extent that they were destroyed. This was mainly due to the fact that they did not know God. But, praise God, the new covenant has this characteristic — that anyone who has eternal life also knows God (John 17:3). Today, eternal life has the function of knowing God. The characteristic of the new covenant is that God gives us revelation and guidance in the law of life. He enables us to worship Him, to serve Him, and to have fellowship with Him, so that we may go on step by step and get to know Him more and more. Now we need to see how in this law of life we can know God without anyone's teaching at all.

THE TEACHING OF THE ANOINTING

Hebrews 8:11 reads: "And they shall by no means teach each one his fellow citizen and each one his brother, saying, Know the Lord, for all shall know Me from the little one to the great among them." The phrase "by no means" is a very strong word in the original text. What is mentioned here coincides with 1 John 2:27: "The anointing which ye received of him abideth in you, and ye need not that any one teach you; but as his anointing teaches you concerning all things, and is true, and is no lie, and even as it taught you, ye abide in him."

The reason why one who has the life of God does not need the teaching of others at all is because he has the Lord's anointing abiding in him, and it teaches him concerning all things. This is a very practical matter. When God's Word says "by no means," it means just that — "by no means." The Lord's anointing always abides in us. It seems the greater the grace is, the more difficult it is for us to believe; therefore, the Word of God says that this anointing "is true" and then follows with the phrase "and is no lie." We should not doubt God's Word simply because our spiritual condition is abnormal. What God says is consistent with what He accomplishes. We need to believe God's Word, and we also need to thank and praise Him.

To properly understand the teaching of the anointing we need to consider the three functions of the human spirit. We have said previously that man's spirit is composed of three parts or functions: intuition, fellowship, and conscience. Let us consider them separately.

The Spirit Has the Function of Fellowship

It is a fact that when we were regenerated, our spirit became alive. To have our spirit made alive is the first step in the fellowship between God and man. We know further that when we were regenerated the Holy Spirit came to dwell in us. We also know that God is Spirit, and that for this reason he who worships Him must worship in spirit and in reality. The Holy Spirit guides man in his spirit to worship God and to have fellowship with God. This shows the function of the fellowship of our human spirit.

The Spirit Has the Function of Conscience

When we were regenerated, our conscience was made alive. The blood of the Lord Jesus purifies the conscience, making it clean and causing its sense to be keen. The Holy Spirit testifies in our conscience concerning our behavior and walk. Romans 8:16 says, "The Spirit Himself witnesses with our spirit." Romans 9:1 says, "My conscience bearing witness with me in the Holy Spirit." First Corinthians 5:3 reveals that the spirit judges, and 2 Corinthians 1:12 says that our conscience testifies. These all indicate that the spirit has the function of conscience.

If we are wrong, the Holy Spirit will condemn us in our conscience. We must pay attention to the fact that what the conscience condemns, God will also condemn. It cannot be that the conscience has condemned something, yet God justifies it. If our conscience says we are wrong, then we must be wrong. Since we are wrong, we must repent, confess, and be cleansed by the Lord's precious blood

(1 John 1:9). If our conscience is pure and void of offence
(2 Tim. 1:3; Acts 24:16), then we can serve God with
boldness and without fear.

The Spirit Has the Function of Intuition

Just as man's body has its senses, man's spirit also has
its senses. The sense of the human spirit is in the
innermost part of man's being. Matthew 26:41 says, "the
spirit indeed is ready." Mark 2:8 says, "perceiving in his
spirit." Mark 8:12 says He "sighed deeply in his spirit."
John 11:33 reads, "He groaned in His spirit." In Acts 17:16
we read, "his spirit was provoked"; in Acts 18:25, "being
fervent in spirit"; in Acts 19:21, "purposed in the spirit";
and in Acts 20:22, "bound in the spirit." Then 1 Corinthians 16:18 says, "they refreshed my spirit," and 2 Corinthians 7:13 says, "his spirit hath been refreshed." These are
all functions of the intuition of the spirit. (It would be right
to say that the senses of the spirit are almost as many as
those of the soul. For this reason we need to learn to
discern what is of the spirit and what is of the soul. Not
until we have gone through the deeper work of the cross
and of the Holy Spirit can we know what is of the spirit
and what is of the soul.)

We call the sense of the spirit "intuition" because it
comes directly from the spirit. Normally, a person's feeling
is aroused by some external factors such as persons,
things, or events. If it is something which should cause
rejoicing, we rejoice; if it is something which should cause
sorrow, we feel sorrowful. Such feelings have their causes;
therefore, we do not call these intuition. The intuition we
are speaking of is the sense which comes directly from
inside man without any apparent cause. For instance, we
may feel like doing something because there is a valid
reason for it. We like to do it, and so we decide to do it. Yet,
for some unknown reason there is an inexplicable feeling
within us which seems to be very heavy and very
depressed. It seems that something inside us is opposing

what we are thinking in our mind, feeling in our emotion, or have decided in our will. Something inside, it seems, is telling us that we should not do it. this is the forbidding of the intuition.

Here is another illustration. Perhaps there is a sense to do something for which there is no reason at all. Besides having no reason, it is contrary to what we desire, and we are not willing to do it. Yet at the same time, for a reason unknown to us, there is a certain kind of urging, moving, and encouraging, wanting us to do it. If we go ahead and do it we will feel comfortable. This is the urging of the intuition.

The Anointing is in the Intuition of the Spirit

The intuition is the place where the anointing teaches us. The Apostle John says, "The anointing which ye received of him abideth in you, and ye need not that any one teach you; but as His anointing teacheth you concerning all things, and is true, and is no lie, and even as it taught you, ye abide in him" (1 John 2:27). This verse clearly shows how the anointing of the Holy Spirit teaches us. The Holy Spirit dwells in our spirit, and the anointing is in the intuition of the spirit.

The Lord's anointing teaches us all things. This means that the Holy Spirit teaches us in the intuition of the spirit, causing us to have some feeling in our spirit, just as when ointment is applied to man's body, causing him to have some sensation. When our spirit has such a feeling, we know what the Holy Spirit says. We need to differentiate between knowing and understanding. We know in our spirit, but we understand with our mind. We know a certain thing through the intuition of the spirit; then the mind is enlightened to understand what the intuition knows. It is in the intuition of the spirit that we know the intention of the Holy Spirit, but it is in the mind of the soul that we understand the guidance of the Holy Spirit.

The work of the anointing is independent and does not

need any human help. Independently it expresses its own intention. It works by itself in the spirit, enabling man to know its intention in the intuition. The Bible calls such knowing in the intuition of the spirit revelation. Revelation means that the Holy Spirit shows the true picture of a thing in our spirit so that we clearly know. This kind of knowing is deeper than the understanding of the mind. The Lord's anointing abides in us and teaches us concerning all things. For this reason we do not need the teaching of others at all. This anointing teaches us in all things through the function of the intuition.

The Holy Spirit expresses Himself through the intuition of the spirit. The intuition is an innate ability to know what the moving of the Holy Spirit means. For this reason, if we want to do God's will, it is not necessary to ask others, nor is it necessary to ask ourselves. We need only to follow the guidance of the intuition. The Lord's anointing teaches us in all things. There is not one instance or one thing concerning which it does not teach us. Therefore, our only responsibility is to receive the teaching of the anointing.

Some Examples

A brother once told the following story. There was a certain Christian, who before being saved, drank very much. This Christian also had a friend who drank in excess. Later both were saved. One day the younger one invited the older one to dinner. Wine was set upon the table. The older one said, "Since we are saved, perhaps we should not drink." The younger one replied, "It doesn't matter if we only take a little, for what we drink is Timothian wine. This is something permitted by the Scriptures." Later they asked a minister of the Word this question, "After a man is saved, should he drink Timothian wine?" The minister replied that he had worked for over ten years and had never heard of anything called Timothian wine. After a few days they came to tell the minister that they were not drinking Timothian wine anymore. When asked by him whether they were taught by someone, they said, "No." They were asked if they were taught by the Scriptures, to which the answer again was no. They said, "As a matter of fact, the Scriptures say that Timothy should use a little wine. But we do not drink because there is a forbidding within." Brothers and sisters, this inner forbidding is the forbidding of the law of life. The law of life is living and powerful, and this law would not allow them to drink. Because the law of life can speak, can work, and can give us feeling, we should respect it.

A servant of God said that a brother came to see him one time, asking whether he should do a certain thing. The servant of God asked, "Do you know inside?" When asked this question he immediately answered, "I know." A few days later he came asking about something else. Again he was asked, "Do you know inside?" To this he replied, "Oh, I know, I know." The third time he came, and the third time he was asked the same question. He immediately said he knew. Although at that time the servant of God did not say so with his mouth, he said in his heart, "Why do you need to take the roundabout way? There is something inside of you which teaches you in all things, and is true and is no lie." This something is the law of life. It will teach us what we should do and what we should not do.

The problem, therefore, lies in whether we are willing to follow this law within us. The question is whether or not our heart is fully turned toward God. If our heart is fully turned toward God, then we do not need others to teach us, for then there is in us something living and real which will teach us. Every child of God has this kind of experience. With some it may be more, with others less, but at least we all have some experience that there is this law of life within us. This law is definitely moving and speaking, and it does not need man's teaching.

Let us give one more example. A certain Christian liked to show hospitality to believers and especially to ministers.

If he came across one, he would invite him over for dinner or give him some gift. On one occasion he was listening to a minister preaching in a certain place. What this man was preaching was not in accordance with the Scripture, for he did not confess that Jesus Christ had come in the flesh. While this brother listened, on the one hand he felt uncomfortable, but on the other hand, according to his habit, he wanted to go shake hands with the minister and say a few words. When he was about to shake hands with him, he sensed something inside forbidding him. He hesitated for a minute. Finally he gave up and went home. This Christian did not realize that 2 John 7-10 says that some call themselves ministers of Christ and yet do not confess that Jesus Christ is come in the flesh. This brother did not know that such a person should not be greeted nor received into one's house, and yet the life inside of him spoke exactly this same thing. This means that while there is absolutely no need for others to teach us, still we can know. This is the characteristic of the new covenant.

Then Why Do the Scriptures Speak of Teaching?

No doubt some one will raise the question, Why then do the Scriptures speak in many places of teaching? For instance, Paul said, "For this cause have I sent unto you Timothy, who is my beloved and faithful child in the Lord, who shall put you in remembrance of my ways which are in Christ, even as I teach everywhere in every church" (1 Cor. 4:17). He also said, "Howbeit in the church I had rather speak five words with my understanding, that I might instruct others also" (1 Cor. 14:19). Many other places also speak of teaching such as Colossians 1:28; 2:22; 3:16; 1 Tim. 2:7; 3:2; 4:11, 13; 5:17; 2 Tim. 2:2, 24; 3:16. How are such passages to be explained? In order to answer this question we must start from our experience and then see what the Scriptures say.

The Speaking Has Been First Going on Inwardly

The Lord's anointing truly is teaching us inwardly. The difficulty is that we cannot hear. Brothers and sisters, we must realize how weak we are. We are so weak that even though God has spoken once, twice, five times, ten times, or even twenty times, we still have not heard. Sometimes we hear but we pretend that we do not. We understand, yet pretend that we have not understood. Our greatest weakness before God is in the matter of hearing. The Lord said, "He who has an ear, let him hear" (Rev. 2:7a). In each of the seven epistles in Revelation it is repeated, "He who has an ear, let him hear." The Scriptures consider hearing to be a very important matter.

When the disciples asked the Lord Jesus why, in speaking to people, He used parables He answered, "Therefore I speak to them in parables, because seeing they do not see, and hearing they do not hear, neither do they understand" (Matt. 13:13). The Lord Jesus also quoted Isaiah 6:9-10 by saying, "Hearing you shall hear and shall by no means understand, and seeing you shall see and by no means perceive; for the heart of this people has grown fat, and with their ears they have heard heavily, and their eyes they have closed; lest at any time they should perceive with the eyes and hear with the ears and understand with the heart and turn around, and I will heal them" (Matt. 13:14-15). These verses show us that the problem is not that there is no teaching within or that there is not the speaking within, but that man purposely would not hear.

Therefore, many times the problem is not that God has not spoken or that man does not have the speaking within, but that man refuses to hear. God has spoken once, twice, five times, or even ten times, yet we still would not hear. Because we would not hear, we could not hear. Because we do not hear, we simply give up hearing. Job 33:14 says, "For God speaketh once, yea twice, though man regardeth it not." This is the very situation of some of God's children.

Those who have problems in the mind, who are

subjective, who are stubborn in their own ways, and who are conservative, are people who do not easily hear. Therefore, whenever we do not hear God's voice and do not have the teaching of the anointing, we need to realize that something must be wrong with us. We must have some problem. The difficulty is never on God's side, it is always on our side. But praise Him, He is patient and continues to speak to man. Job 33:15-16 says, "In a dream, in a vision of the night, when deep sleep falleth upon men, in slumberings upon the bed; then He openeth the ears of men, and sealeth their instruction." If we do not hear Him, He will still use visions and dreams to instruct us. Therefore, it is not that God has said nothing; God has spoken a great deal. The difficulty is that man is very short in hearing.

Outward Repetition

When we read the Epistles in the New Testament, we realize that many teachings are repetitions. They were repeated because of some difficulties in the church. In the Epistles of the New Testament we often find the phrase, "Know ye not?" Such a phrase appears in Romans 6:3, 16; 1 Corinthians 3:16; 5:6; 6:2-3, 9, 15-16, 19; and James 4:4. "Know ye not" means that though we had heard something and we had known something inside, we had ignored it. We had simply let it go. Therefore, through the Scriptures God says, "Know ye not?" The Scriptures do not speak in place of the anointing within, but simply repeat what the anointing has already said. Because we are spiritually sick and abnormal, and because we have neglected the inner teaching, the Lord through His servant uses the words of the Scriptures, repeating outwardly what the anointing has spoken inwardly. The Lord's anointing has taught us inwardly, so we must start listening from within. We must see that the inward teaching and the outward teaching are mutually helpful. The outward teaching, however, must not replace that which is inward.

The inward speaking is living and of life. This is the characteristic of the new covenant. Everyone who belongs to God must pay attention to this matter.

Here we must say a few words by way of reminder to the brothers and sisters. When we help others we should never give them the "Ten Commandments." Neither should we subjectively teach them to do this or to refrain from that. We should not speak of God's will to individuals as the prophets in the Old Testament did. The reason for this is that in the New Testament the prophets are only for the church and not for individuals. A prophet in the New Testament time can only point out God's ordained will in principle. He should not point out God's will for an individual. All of us who belong to God must learn to receive the teaching of the anointing within, otherwise it is not the new covenant. We can only confirm what God has already spoken in man. All we can do is repeat what God has already taught within. To go further is to go beyond the new covenant. On the other hand we should humbly receive the teaching of those who teach us in the Lord. However, the teaching which we receive must also be the teaching of the anointing within us. Otherwise, it is not the new covenant. We must remember that the letter kills; only the Spirit gives life (2 Cor. 3:6).

The Mind Must be Renewed

The Lord's anointing is in the intuition of our spirit and it teaches us concerning all things, but sometimes our mind cannot understand the sense in the spirit. For this reason our mind must be renewed. Only then can we understand what the anointing is teaching us. Romans 12:2 shows us that first the mind must be renewed and transformed; then we can prove what is God's good, well-pleasing, and perfect will. Colossians 1:9 shows us that we must first have the spiritual understanding; then we will be filled with the full knowledge of God's will. Therefore, the renewing of the mind is essential. If our

mind is not renewed, we can neither know nor understand
the teaching of the anointing. On the other hand, if our
mind is not renewed we will consider the sudden thoughts,
those shot into our mind like lightning, as if they were the
Lord's guidance in us. We will also consider the groundless
ideas and the vain theories as if they were the Lord's will.
We will consider the senseless and worthless visions and
dreams as if they were words which the Lord has spoken to
us and as revelation from Him. These are harmful and of
no benefit.

We admit and believe that the Lord sometimes opens
ears through visions and dreams like that mentioned in
Job 33:15-16, but we do not accept nor believe that confusing thoughts, or senseless and worthless visions and
dreams are of the Lord. Therefore, the renewing of the
mind is very crucial in understanding the teaching of the
anointing. Now the question is: How can the mind be
renewed? Titus 3:5 speaks of the renewing of the Holy
Spirit. Romans 12:1-2 makes it clear that first we must
present our bodies as a living sacrifice; then we may be
transformed by the renewing of the mind. We see from this
that the renewing of the mind is based upon consecration.
Ephesians 4:22-23 shows us that for the renewing of the
spirit of the mind we must, in our experience, first put off
the old man regarding our former manner of life. This
shows that the renewing of the mind is something which is
done through the cross. Ephesians 4:23 says, "And are
renewed in the spirit of your mind." It is clear, therefore,
that the renewing starts from the spirit and then spreads
into the mind. We have said before that the work of the
Holy Spirit starts from the center and spreads to the
circumference. If there is a problem in man's heart, that is,
in the deepest part of him, and it is not dealt with, then it
is impossible to have the mind renewed. Therefore, the
Holy Spirit first renews the spirit of the mind and then
renews the mind.

In summary, because of God's constraining we present

our bodies as a living sacrifice. Following that, the Holy
Spirit through the cross causes us in our experience to
exercise our will to put off the old man concerning his
former manner of life, so that through His life entering
more fully into us, our spirit may be renewed and our mind
may also be renewed. This renewing is a prolonged and
continuous work of the Holy Spirit. When we come to this
point, we need to thank and praise God that everything is
the work of His grace. We have nothing else to do except to
receive His grace and to praise and thank Him. We say
again that the Lord's anointing is in us, teaching us in all
things. This is a true and definite matter. The law of life in
us does not need any man's teaching at all. This is not an
overstatement. The Scripture has indeed said so. But on
the other hand we need to prevent ourselves from being
deceived and from going to extremes. We need to check our
inner feelings by the words in the Scriptures.

Checking Our Inner Feeling by the Scriptures

The Holy Spirit is the Spirit of truth (John 14:17). He
guides us into all the truth (John 16:13). Therefore, if our
inner sense is of the Holy Spirit, this sense must
correspond with what the Scriptures say. If the inner sense
does not match the words of the Scriptures, this sense is
inaccurate. We know that the inner sense is living, and we
also know that the Scriptures without are accurate. If we
merely have the words of the Scripture, there is accuracy
and security, but no life. On the other hand, having merely
the inner sense may be living, but not accurate; or it may
be living, but not secure. Our experience needs to be like a
train which has power inside the locomotive and rails
outside. If there are only rails without but no power within
the locomotive, the train will not move. On the other hand,
if there is only power within the locomotive but no rails
without, the train will run without control and have an
accident. The Scriptures show us that when the Israelites
came out of Egypt, they had before them the pillar of cloud

as their guide in the day and the pillar of fire as their guide in the night. When our spiritual condition is normal, we are walking in the bright daylight. But our spiritual condition is not always like this. The Scriptures also say that God's Word is a lamp unto our feet and a light unto our path (Psa. 119:105). Without the night there is no need for the lamp and the light. When we are bright within, our inner sense is clear and sure. When we are dark within, our inner sense is blurry and uncertain. Then we must use the words of the Scriptures to verify our inner sense.

Life plus truth equals real power. Life and truth result in secure strength. We need to walk upon the secure path of life and truth. Every action, every thought, and every decision needs to be checked against the words in the Scriptures, so that we may go on without being sidetracked.

Two Ways of Knowing God

Let us read Hebrews 8:11 again: "And they shall by no means teach each one his fellow citizen and each one his brother, saying, Know the Lord, for all shall know Me from the little one to the great among them." This verse tells us that we who are God's people in the law of life can know God without any man's teaching. This verse twice uses the word "know." The first time it speaks of men teaching each other to know the Lord. The second time it mentions that from the little one to the great all shall know the Lord. The first knowing signifies the ordinary knowledge; the second knowing refers to knowledge in the intuition. The ordinary knowledge is the objective, outward knowledge, while the intuitive knowledge is the subjective, inward knowledge.

We can illustrate the difference between ordinary knowledge and intuitive knowledge in the following way. Suppose sugar and salt are put before us. They both appear about the same. Both are white and fine, but when they are put into our mouth we know which is sugar and which is salt. The sugar has the taste of sugar, and the salt has the taste of salt. Although we may use our eyes to know the sugar and the salt from without, it is not as accurate as tasting them with our tongue.

Our knowledge of God is the same. The outward knowledge is only an ordinary knowledge, but the inward knowledge is the accurate knowledge. When God gives us a taste of Himself in us, we experience unspeakable joy. Psalm 34:8 says, "Oh taste and see that Jehovah is good." It is wonderful! We can taste God! Hebrews 6:4-5 mentions: "... those who were once enlightened, and who have tasted of the heavenly gift, and have become partakers of the Holy Spirit, and have tasted the good word of God, and the works of power of the coming age." This shows us that the spiritual things need to be tasted. Thank God that the characteristic of the new covenant not only enables us to taste spiritual things; it even enables us to taste God Himself. What a great blessing and what a great glory this is!

Three Steps in Knowing God

According to the Scriptures, man's knowing God can be divided into three steps. Psalm 103:7 says, "He made known his ways unto Moses, His doings unto the children of Israel." The word "ways" in this verse is the same word used in Isaiah 55:8. The Israelites only knew God's doings, but Moses knew God's ways. It is clear that Moses' knowing of God was more advanced than that of the children of Israel. But the knowing in the intuition, mentioned in Hebrews 8:11, is more advanced than knowing God's ways. The knowing in the intuition is to know God's nature, to know God Himself. If we read these last two verses of Scripture together, we can see that our knowing God can be divided into three steps. The first step is to know God's doings; the second step is to know God's ways; and the third step is to know God Himself. To know God's doings and ways are only outward knowing, but the inward knowing of God's nature and knowing God Himself is the deeper knowing. This is the most precious. Now let us look at these three steps separately.

Knowing God's Doings

To know God's doings means to know the miracles and wonders which He performs. The children of Israel in the land of Egypt, for instance, saw the ten plagues which God sent (Exo. 7—11). Another example is when God sent the great east wind, causing the water of the Red Sea to recede in one night, so that the water was divided and the sea became dry ground (Exo. 14:21). Two other examples are: the children of Israel obtaining living water from the smitten rock in the wilderness (Exo. 17:6) and the daily manna sent down from heaven (Exo. 16:35). All of these were God's doings. Likewise, the feeding of the five thousand with five loaves and two fishes (John 6:9-12), the blind receiving sight, the lame walking, the lepers being cleansed, the deaf hearing, and the dead being raised (Matt. 11:5) were all God's doings. Today some people have been healed of their illness by God, or have been protected by God from danger on a journey. These are all God's doings. But if we only know God's doings, we cannot be considered as knowing God. This kind of knowing is shallow and outward.

Knowing God's Ways

To know God's ways means to know the principle by which God does things. For example, when Abraham prayed for Sodom, he prayed by standing on the side of God's righteousness. He knew that because God is a righteous God, He could not act contrary to His righteousness. This means that Abraham knew God's way of doing things. Another example can be seen in the incident where Moses saw the glory of Jehovah manifested, and told Aaron, "Take thy censer, and put fire therein from off the altar, and lay incense thereon, and carry it quickly unto the congregation, and make atonement for them: for there is wrath gone out from Jehovah; the plague is begun" (Num. 16:46). This means that Moses knew God's ways. He knew that if man would act in a certain way, then God would respond in a certain way.

Samuel told Saul: "Behold, to obey is better than sacrifice, and to hearken than the fat of rams" (1 Sam. 15:22). This refers to knowing God's ways. A further example is when David refused to offer burnt offerings which cost him nothing (2 Sam. 24:24). This also refers to knowing God's ways.

Knowing God Himself

To know God's nature means to know God Himself. It has been mentioned before that every kind of life has its own characteristics. Fish have the characteristics of fish and birds have the characteristics of birds. God's life also has its characteristic. This characteristic is His nature. His nature is goodness, uprightness (Psa. 25:8; 86:5; Matt. 19:17) and holiness (Acts 3:14; 2 Cor. 1:12). This nature will express God Himself through light. When we are born again we obtain God's life and receive God's nature. When we touch His nature in us, we also touch God Himself in us. This is knowing God Himself. For instance, if there is some sin, our conscience feels that it must be dealt with, and only if it is dealt with can there be peace. Yet, inside of us there is a holy sense, a sense which is even deeper than the conscience. Deep within there is a disgust and a hatred for the sin itself. This kind of hatred comes from God's holy nature. When man touches God Himself, his knowledge of God's holiness is beyond human description. Sometimes our sensation is the same as Job's: "I had heard of thee by the hearing of the ear; but now mine eye seeth thee: wherefore I abhor myself and repent in dust and ashes" (Job. 42:5-6).

Under the bright sunlight even the dust will be revealed. Likewise, in God's holiness, our filthiness is always revealed. No wonder that when Peter met the Lord Himself, he fell down at the Lord's knees and said, "Depart from me; for I am a sinful man, O Lord" (Luke 5:8). Many times, both in our words and in our actions, although our conscience may not condemn us, there is still within a sense of discomfort, a sense which does not say "amen." This is the sense of the nature of God's life, and it exceeds the feeling of the conscience. If we have learned and are willing to obey, it is at such times that we touch God Himself. On these occasions we will know God Himself.

Paul told the Corinthian believers, "We toil, working with our own hands: being reviled, we bless; being persecuted, we endure; being defamed, we entreat: we are made as the filth of the world, the offscouring of all things, even until now" (1 Cor. 4:12-13). This shows that not only is God's life such, but it also shows that the nature of this life is such. When Paul was so touching God's nature he was touching God Himself. It was then that he knew God Himself.

The following is a true story. Two brothers who were farmers and also Christians planted rice fields. The fields were in the middle of a hill. Every day the brothers pumped the water into the fields with their feet. But every day they found that the farmer whose field was below them always used subtle ways to let the water out of their fields into his field below. For seven or eight days they endured this without saying a word, but inside there was not the joy. Later, they went to have fellowship with a brother who was a servant of the Lord. He told them, "It is not enough for you to endure. You should go and also water the field of him who stole your water. Then pump the water for your own fields." The two brothers went back to their fields and did as he had spoken. It was strange — the more they did this, the more they felt happy. The result was that the one who stole the water was touched. Not only did he

no longer come to steal their water, but he came to
apologize to them. Here we see that the reason they could
do this, and do it so spontaneously, was because they did it
according to God's nature. Otherwise, if they did it only in
an outward way, inwardly they would still have the feeling
they were being wronged. Later they would still feel
distressed within. Only the things which are done
according to God's nature make us feel comfortable inside.
The more we do things this way, the more we will praise
God, and the more we will know God Himself.

Knowing God in Our Intuition

To know God Himself is the greatest blessing and the
greatest glory in the new covenant. God Himself cannot be
known by the flesh, but only by the intuition. Let us see
what the Scriptures say about knowing God in our
intuition. John 17:3 says: "And this is eternal life, that
they may know You, the only true God, and Him Whom
You have sent, Jesus Christ." This verse tells us that every
one who has eternal life knows God and the Lord Jesus. In
other words, when a man receives eternal life he receives a
knowing of God in the intuition which he did not possess
before. This eternal life has a function which enables man
to know God. We know God, the One who has been made
known to us, by the life within. We are not like the people
of Athens who, by reasoning and inference, worshipped an
unknown God (Acts 17:23). Therefore, if someone says that
he has eternal life and yet has never known God, then his
claim to have eternal life is doubtful — it is only in the
letter. To put it even stronger, this kind of person does not
have eternal life. If we want to know God we must first
have eternal life.

First Corinthians 2:11-12 says, "For who among men
knoweth the things of a man, save the spirit of man,
which is in him? even so the things of God none knoweth,
save the Spirit of God. But we received, not the spirit of the
world, but the spirit which is from God; that we might

know the things that were freely given to us of God." This verse tells us that it is the Holy Spirit, who is in our spirit, who enables us to know the things of God. The things of God cannot be known by man's mind; man cannot figure them out by his own thoughts, nor can he comprehend them by his own wisdom. Therefore, the Scriptures say, "Now the natural man receiveth not the things of the Spirit of God: for they are foolishness unto him; and he cannot know them" (1 Cor. 2:14).

Ephesians 1:17-18 says, "That the God of our Lord Jesus Christ, the Father of glory, may give to you a spirit of wisdom and revelation in the full knowledge of Him, the eyes of your heart having been enlightened, that you may know ..." These verses tell us that the Apostle prayed for the believers at Ephesus who had been regenerated, that they might receive the spirit of wisdom and revelation, and that they might have the full knowledge of God in their intuition. Whether this spirit of wisdom and revelation is a function which has been hidden in the spirit of the believer and which will be uncovered by God through prayer, or whether it is through prayer that the Holy Spirit causes the believer to receive anew the wisdom and revelation in his spirit, is difficult to say; in any case, this spirit of wisdom and revelation enables the believer to have the full knowledge of God. Our intuition needs wisdom and revelation. We need wisdom to know what is of God and what is of ourselves. We need wisdom to know the false apostles and the false angels of light (2 Cor. 11:13-14). When God gives us wisdom, He does not give it to our mind, but He gives it to our spirit. God wants us to have wisdom in our intuition. He wants to lead us to the path of wisdom through intuition. We need revelation to truly know Him. The spirit of revelation means that God moves in our spirit and enables our intuition to know the intent of God and to know God's movement. It is only by receiving revelation in the spirit that we can have the full knowledge of God.

When God gives us the spirit of wisdom and revelation
He not only causes us to have the full knowledge of Him in
our intuition, but He also enlightens the eyes of our heart.
The eyes of our heart here refers to our understanding, the
dianoia, found in Ephesians 4:18. This is simply the
faculty of perception and understanding. In Ephesians
1:17-18 two knowings are mentioned. The first one is the
knowing of the intuition, while the second is the knowing
or the understanding of the mind. The spirit of revelation
is in the deepest part of our being. God reveals Himself in
our spirit so that we may have a full knowledge of Him
through the intuition. This knowing, however, is only the
knowing in the intuition — only the inner man knows; the
outer man still does not know. Our spirit still needs to
enlighten our mind with light so that our mind can
understand the intent of the spirit, bringing the outer man
to know as well. Therefore, revelation begins in the spirit,
and then it arrives at the mind. Revelation is in the
intuition of the spirit, while enlightenment is in the mind
of the soul. In the intuition we know by sensing, while in
the mind we understand by seeing. Thus, God gives us the
spirit of wisdom and revelation, that we may truly know
Him and truly understand Him.

Colossians 1:9-10 says, "... that you may be filled with
the full knowledge of His will in all spiritual wisdom and
understanding, to walk worthily of the Lord unto all
pleasing, bearing fruit in every good work and growing by
the full knowledge of God." This passage shows us that we
need to have spiritual wisdom and understanding in order
to know God's will, to do the things which are pleasing to
Him, and to have the full knowledge of Him. We have seen
that it is God who gives us spiritual wisdom in our spirit,
but at the same time we must also have the spiritual
understanding to understand the revelation which God has
given to us in the intuition of our spirit. On the one hand,
the intuition of the spirit enables us to know God's
movement, while on the other hand, spiritual understand-

ing enables us to know the meaning of the movement in
our spirit. If in all things we seek God's will in our spirit,
the result will be that more and more we will know God
Himself. We will grow by the full knowledge of God. This
will cause our intuition to grow indefinitely. The growth of
the intuition is simply the growth of life. The more the life
grows, the more God will occupy us. Therefore, we must go
along with the moving of the law of life and train our spirit
to know God in a deeper way. What we need is the full
knowledge of Him. We must ask God to give us the spirit of
wisdom and revelation, and to give us spiritual understanding, so that day by day we may grow by the full
knowledge of God.

Matthew 5:8 says, "Blessed are the pure in heart, for
they shall see God." Here again we see the matter of the
heart. If our heart is pure and not doubleminded, as
mentioned in James 4:8, we shall see God. If our heart
desires and covets things other than God Himself, there
will be a veil inside. Thus our perception of God will be
blurred. Therefore, whenever we feel blurry inside, the
most important thing to do is to ask God to show us
whether or not our heart is pure.

The Lord Jesus said, "If anyone loves Me, he will keep
My word, and My Father will love him, and We will come
to him and make an abode with him" (John 14:23). This
verse tells us that if we love and obey the Lord, God will
make an abode with us. God will give us the sense of His
presence. This corresponds with 1 John 2:27 where we are
told to abide in the Lord according to the teaching of the
anointing. This means that when we walk according to the
teaching of the anointing, we keep the Lord's word. Then
we will abide in the Lord and God will make an abode with
us. This kind of obedience issues forth out of our love
toward God and not out of coercion by others.

Brother Lawrence said that if our heart can in any
measure come to know God, it can do so only through love.
He also said that the pleasures of man's heart are different

from his sentiments. The proper outlet of sentiments is love, and the object of love is God. Therefore, we should sing:

> What e'er thou lovest, man,
> That too become thou must;
> God, if thou lovest God,
> Dust, if thou lovest dust.
> Go out, God will come in;
> Die thou and let Him live;
> Be not and He will be;
> Wait and He'll all things give.
>
> > O, Cross of Christ, I take thee
> > Into this heart of mine,
> > That I to my own self may die
> > And rise to Thy life Divine.
>
> To bring thee to thy God,
> Love takes the shortest route;
> The way which knowledge leads,
> Is but a roundabout.
> Drive out from thee the world,
> And then thy heart shall be
> Filled with the love of God,
> And holy like as He.

(Hymns, 477)

Love is surely the most proper outlet of sentiments. Love is not reluctant. We love God because He first loved us (1 John 4:19). The more we love Him, the more we will draw close to Him. The more we draw close to Him, the more we will know Him. The more we know Him, the more we will love Him, and the more we will long after Him.

The saints of old wrote in the Psalms: "As the hart panteth after the water brooks, so panteth my soul after thee, O God" (Psa. 42:1). This is the longing of those who have tasted God. One of the Lord's children has said that God gave us a heart which is so great that only He can fill it. We perhaps thought that our heart was small, but those

who have tasted God will testify that the heart is so big
that it cannot be filled by anything less than God Himself.
Only God can fill our heart. Brothers and sisters, how
much does your heart long after God?

The Outward Expression of God

Our outward expression of God cannot exceed our
inward knowledge. The degree of our inward knowledge of
God determines the extent of our outward expression of
Him. In other words, the outward expression is the result
of inward knowledge. Now let us consider some different
aspects of this matter.

Expression in Boldness and Discernment

The Apostle Paul said, "But when it pleased God, Who
set me apart from my mother's womb and called me
through His grace, to reveal His Son in me, that I might
preach Him among the nations, immediately I did not
confer with flesh and blood, neither did I go up to
Jerusalem to those who were apostles before me" (Gal.
1:15-17). This shows that the reason Paul had the boldness
to preach the gospel to the nations was because his
knowledge of the Son of God was by revelation. This kind
of knowledge cannot be obtained through the flesh.

When a person knows Christ in himself, he will also
know Christ in others. This is what Paul had in mind
when he said, "We henceforth know no man after the
flesh" (2 Cor. 5:16). Those who know men according to the
flesh find it rather difficult to receive the life supply from
men. They are easily affected by the shortcomings in
men's appearance. If there is any flaw in others, it becomes
material for them to criticize and judge, and it also
becomes the element for them to nourish their own pride.
Therefore, whether a person can know Christ in others
depends upon whether he knows Christ in himself. Paul
continued, "Even though we have known Christ after the
flesh, yet now we know him so no more" (2 Cor. 5:16). The

Apostle John said, "And every spirit that confesseth not Jesus is not of God: and this is the spirit of the antichrist, ... Ye are of God, my little children, and have overcome them: because greater is he that is in you than he that is in the world" (1 John 4:3-4). Those who truly know God can discern the false apostles (2 Cor. 11:13; Rev. 2:2), the false prophets (Matt. 24:11), the false brethren (2 Cor. 11:26; Gal. 2:4), and the false angels of light (2 Cor. 11:13-15). Whenever we are deceived it must be because we do not know men by Christ, who is in us. Those who truly know God have the boldness to declare, "Greater is He who dwells in us than the spirit of antichrist!"

Expression in the Fear of God

One who truly knows God, not only has the boldness to testify, and is not afraid of the spirit of antichrist, but he especially fears God. For example, the steps Paul took in his work were, many times, forbidden by God (Acts 16:6-7). He feared God. Another example of his fear of God is given in Acts 23:3-5, when being reminded that he rebuked the high priest, he became softened. This means that he feared God.

Those who truly know God gird up the loins of their mind (1 Pet. 1:13). There is nothing loose in their words, attitude, and actions. The reason they are so girded up is not because they have some strength of their own, but because the life in them is restraining them and forbidding them. They are such not only before others, but even when they are by themselves they are girded up. Whenever their words and actions do not match the life in them, those words and actions are forbidden. Also, whenever they touch God they become softened.

Those who are loose outwardly must first be loose inwardly. Those who are loose and without restraint, who remain the same after being saved, who are careless in what they say and in what they do, are Christians who do not fear God. Those who act one way in front of people and another way behind their backs, who are one way in the pulpit and another way in daily living, are those who do not fear God.

To fear God means that anywhere, at any time, in any activity, we dare not be loose. Within there is the attitude of fearing God. Therefore, if someone claims to belong to God, and yet his words and his actions do not indicate that he fears God in the least, we will have a genuine concern for such a person. We fear for him because the day will come when he will see God's face, though today he does not know God in his consciousness. Brothers and sisters, if this is your case, then you need to hear God's word: "And now, my little children, abide in him; that, if he shall be manifested, we may have boldness, and not be ashamed before him at his coming" (1 John 2:28).

Whenever we think of the fact that one day we shall see the Lord's face, do we feel confident within? In the future, when everything shall be opened before the Lord, will there be anything which will cause us to be ashamed?

Expression in Worship

There is no one who truly knows God, yet does not worship God. Brother Lawrence said, "To worship God in truth is to acknowledge Him to be what He is, and ourselves as what in very fact we are. To worship Him in truth is to acknowledge with heartfelt sincerity what God in truth is — that is to say, infinitely perfect, worthy of infinite adoration, infinitely removed from sin, and so of all the Divine attributes. That man is little guided by reason, who does not employ all his powers to render to this great God the worship that is His due."

This indicates that only the person who truly knows God can worship God in truth. For example, though Jacob's knowledge of God at Bethel caused him to fear God, it was only an outward kind of knowledge. For this reason his vow was conditional and was concerned with his own interests (Gen. 28:16-22). But when he came to

Peniel (Gen. 32:24-32), Jacob's knowledge of God was much different.

Brothers and sisters, we often say that we need to worship God. But how deeply have we ourselves known God? Has our self really fallen to the ground?

Expression in Godliness

Those who truly know God will express God. This is the life of godliness. Godliness itself is a great mystery. From the time God was manifested in the flesh (1 Tim. 3:16), this great mystery has been revealed. Oh, Jesus the Nazarene was God being manifested in the flesh! This glorious One who is both God and man has manifested God's holy and glorious life. Today, this life is in us and it will also be manifested through us. The purpose of the law of God's life moving in us is to fulfill this requirement. We know that godliness is not some kind of mortification but rather a sense of life. Godliness is the nature of God's life. Therefore, when the Apostle Paul said that those who belong to the Lord should pursue righteousness, godliness, faith, love, endurance, and meekness, he included godliness (1 Tim. 6:11).

When we were regenerated, God, according to His divine power, gave to us all things that pertain to life and godliness (2 Pet. 1:3). Also, this godliness has the promise of the present life and of the life which is coming (1 Tim. 4:8). We know that what the Lord promises us is eternal life (1 John 2:25; Titus 1:2). When we believe in the Son of God, we receive this eternal life (1 John 5:13). However, to live out this eternal life today, to express this eternal life in our thoughts, words, attitude, and actions, depends upon the power of the moving of this life within us. Therefore, the Apostle Paul said: "We have set our hope on the living God, Who is the Savior of all men, especially of those who believe" (1 Tim. 4:10).

Within us we already have the godly life of God, but to manifest the nature of this life, we need to exercise

ourselves unto godliness (1 Tim. 4:7). We know that fear of
God is a matter of attitude. This means that we are afraid
of having our self in anything we do. We are afraid to sin
against God. On the other hand, godliness means that we
let God come forth in everything we do. To exercise
ourselves unto godliness, on the negative side, means to
deny all ungodliness (Titus 2:12), things which do not
conform to God. On the positive side, we need to let God
come forth in everything. This kind of godliness is not
some kind of mortification. It is not a matter of closing the
doors and ignoring everything, but it is a matter of abiding
in the Lord according to the teaching of the anointing, and
learning to let the law of life manifest the nature of God's
life in our daily life (1 Tim. 2:2). This kind of exercising
unto godliness is more profitable than bodily exercise.

Although today we cannot experience this eternal life
completely, if we experience it day by day, one day we will
be completely like Him when our body has been redeemed,
and we will fully enjoy this eternal life. This is God's
eternal purpose. This is the glory of the new covenant. We
need to praise the Lord with a heart full of expectation.

We also need to realize that there is one thing which is
unavoidable to all that would live godly in Christ Jesus.
Paul told Timothy, "But you have closely followed my
teaching, conduct, purpose, faith, longsuffering, love,
endurance, persecutions, sufferings, which happened to me
in Antioch, in Iconium, in Lystra; what persecutions I bore
..." (2 Tim. 3:10-11). Someone might think that it was
because Paul was an apostle that he could not avoid such
persecutions, but Paul continued, "And indeed, all who
desire to live godly in Christ Jesus will be persecuted"
(v. 12).

Not only can an apostle not avoid persecution, but,
without exception, any one who is determined to live godly
in Christ Jesus will also be persecuted. If in our daily life
we will be just a little accommodating, a little complacent,
a little clever and tactful, wise to protect ourselves, go

along with the worldly customs, mingle with others, give in concerning the truths, and compromise with those who are not willing to pay the price; if we would just please others at the cost of truth, not seeking the inner voice, and not obeying the inner sense, then we may be a Christian, but we will be a Christian without persecution. For who would persecute us if we are the same as everyone else?

We should not think that those Christians who have suffered much persecutions are those who have the ill fortune to be born at the wrong time and who have been destined to encounter oppositions. On the contrary, the fact is that those Christians who do not suffer persecution are the ones who would not live godly in Christ Jesus; otherwise, persecution would be unavoidable. For this reason a believer once said, "The most spiritual believers are seamed with scars; martyrs have put on their crown glittering with fire." But we need not be fearful, for either the Lord will empower us, making us able to endure, or He will deliver us from all the sufferings (1 Cor. 10:13; 2 Cor. 1:8-10; 2 Tim. 3:11).

Here also we need to mention that exercising unto godliness, or living godly in Christ Jesus, is a spiritual pursuit and an overflow of life. Some manifestations of such exercise are normal and need not be mentioned here. But we will mention certain manifestations which may be considered sick conditions and which are defects.

1. Laziness

Some Christians, it seems, were born lazy. They neither like to labor nor to work. They use prayer and spiritual words as a shelter for their laziness. A brother told us of a certain sister who did not like to do things. Either she would have the excuse of not knowing how to do it or she would have the excuse of not having the strength to do it. At one point someone arranged for her to pick some flowers from the garden every day and arrange them in a vase. After a few days she stopped doing it, saying that it was not spiritual. This is a sick condition. This is not godliness.

2. Rigidness

Some Christians think that godliness means to be rigid. Such rigidness makes them appear artificial. One brother met a certain one who, whenever he would say a few words, would bow down his head, or raise up his head to look up into the heavens. This person was pretending to be godly. The brother who related this incident said he felt like shouting to him, "Brother, stop this nonsense!" We know what life is; it is spontaneous. It is hard for the spirit of a rigid person to come forth, and so God cannot come forth either. Therefore, whenever we exercise ourselves unto godliness, we should be living and fresh. It must be God who comes forth in our words and in our attitude.

3. Coldness

We mentioned previously, that if we live godly in Christ Jesus we will be persecuted. This means that those who will not sin against God in order to please men will encounter persecutions. This is not to say, however, that we may be negligent in love and in courtesy toward others.

A certain sister was taking a walk in the mountains. There came another sister who greeted her and asked where she was going. She looked up into the heavens and coldly answered, "I am going to see God." Let us not think that such a self-assumed godliness and such a cold, hard-hearted attitude will ever attract others to long after God.

4. Passiveness

Some Christians who admire Madame Guyon and Brother Lawrence (who practiced the presence of God) seek to practice godliness as they did. This is something to be respected. It is even desirable. However, unfortunately, there are others who imitate them and become passive. Why do we say that they learn yet fall into passivity?

Because they often cannot hear what others say. It is right to ignore people's gossip, but to ignore the important things said by others is an insult to them. Those who practice godliness and become passive also cannot understand what others say, nor show any concern for the affairs of others. Yet they think they are enjoying the presence of God. If this were normal, then how could Brother Lawrence handle the affairs in the midst of the noise and clatter of his busy environment? If someone asked him for a plate and he gave them a spoon, if he could not hear their first request nor understand their repeated request, would it not be a hardship for others? Therefore, we must say that it is not normal to practice godliness by being passive.

Brothers and sisters, our Lord is the Word who became flesh and tabernacled among us, full of grace and reality (John 1:14). This is a great revelation of godliness. Paul, who told Timothy that only godliness is profitable for all things (1 Tim. 4:8), is the one who said, "Who is weak, and I am not weak? who is caused to stumble, and I burn not?" (2 Cor. 11:29). He also worked with his own hands (1 Cor. 4:12), and he labored more abundantly than all the apostles (1 Cor. 15:10). Oh, brothers and sisters, this is our example. We should respect Paul and learn of him.

A Hymn of Prayer

To exercise ourselves unto godliness is to let this godly life express itself and become a godly living, until one day we shall be completely like God. There is a hymn of prayer which properly expresses this pursuit. We print it here as our prayer.

> O to be like thee! blessed Redeemer;
> This is my constant longing and prayer;
> Gladly I'll forfeit all of earth's treasures,
> Jesus, Thy perfect likeness to wear.
>
> O to be like Thee! O to be like Thee!
> Blessed Redeemer, pure as Thou art;

Come in Thy sweetness, come in Thy fullness;
Stamp Thine own image deep on my heart.

O to be like Thee! full of compassion,
Loving, forgiving, tender and kind,
Helping the helpless, cheering the fainting,
Seeking the wand'ring sinners to find.

O to be like Thee! lowly in spirit,
Holy and harmless, patient and brave;
Meekly enduring cruel reproaches,
Willing to suffer, others to save.

O to be like Thee! Lord, I am coming,
Now to receive th' anointing divine;
All that I am and have I am bringing;
Lord, from this moment all shall be Thine.

O to be like Thee! While I am pleading
Pour out Thy Spirit, fill with Thy love.
Make me a temple meet for Thy dwelling,
Fit for a life which Thou wouldst approve.

(*Hymns,* 398)

The Need for God's Continual Forgiveness and Cleansing

The power of God's life will fulfill God's eternal purpose in us. Today, upon the earth, we have the promise of God's life which is godliness. This does not mean that we are complete to such an extent that we no longer need confession, no longer need· God's forgiveness, and no longer need the cleansing of the precious blood. No! We must read Hebrews 8:12 again: "For I will be propitious to their unrighteousnesses, and their sins I will by no means remember anymore."

In the sixth chapter of this book we pointed out that we must pay attention to the word "for" in this verse. It is very important, for it shows that God being propitious toward our unrighteousnesses and by no means remembering our sins anymore is the cause; but that God has imparted His laws into our mind and has inscribed them upon our hearts and has become our God in the law of life and has made us His people in the law of life for this purpose: that we might have a deeper knowledge of Him. To know God is the purpose, so it is mentioned first; but the forgiveness of sins is the procedure, so it is mentioned later.

A similar instance can be found in Ephesians 1. First, in verse 5, we are told that God "predestinated us unto sonship through Jesus Christ to Himself," because this is the purpose. Later, in verse 7, it is mentioned that "we have redemption through His blood, the forgiveness of offenses," because this is the procedure.

Before God can give us His life, He must forgive us and cleanse us of our sins. This also indicates that after we have God's life, if we have sin and do not deal with it, it will hinder the growth of this life. Therefore, in order for God's life to move within us without hindrance, we must not tolerate sin. Sin must be confessed to God and forgiveness must be obtained. We may also need to confess to others and ask for their forgiveness.

We should not think that we can exercise unto godliness to such an extent that we no longer need God's forgiveness or the cleansing of the precious blood. On the contrary, the more one knows God, the more he feels the poverty of his condition and the more he will confess before God, seeking forgiveness, and the more he will experience the cleansing of the blood. Often those Christians whom we consider to be most holy are ones who have shed many tears before God. For it is in God's light that we see light (Psa. 36:9), and in God's light we will see our real condition. Our hidden flesh and our hidden self will be exposed in God's light. At such a time we will truly say to God: "I will declare mine iniquity; I will be sorry for my sin" (Psa. 38:18). We will also say to God: "Clear thou me from hidden faults. Keep back thy servant also from presumptuous sins.... Let the words of my mouth and the meditation of my heart be acceptable in thy sight, O Jehovah, my rock, and my redeemer" (Psa. 19:12-14, lit.).

A servant of God once gave a word based upon 1 John 1

in which he pointed out that life requires fellowship and also brings in fellowship; fellowship brings in light; and light requires the blood. Here we notice a series of experiences. If a person has life he will seek fellowship; when there is fellowship he will see light; and when he sees light he will seek the blood. These four things not only constitute a series, they also are causally related to each other. Life causes us to have fellowship, and fellowship imparts life to us. Fellowship causes us to see light, and light brings a deeper fellowship. Light prompts us to seek the cleansing of the blood, and the cleansing of the blood allows us to see the light more clearly. These four items not only are causally related to each other, but they are also in a cycle, with life bringing us to fellowship; fellowship causing us to see light; light causing us to receive the cleansing of the blood; and following the cleansing of the blood the receiving of more life. When we receive more life, we will have more fellowship, and when we have more fellowship we will see more light; then having seen more light we will receive more cleansing of the blood. These four items recur thus in a cycle. The experience of this cycle will cause us to move ahead in life.

As a car moves by the continuous turning of the wheels, so the experience of these four matters is just like the turning of the wheels. Whenever a cycle is completed, we move on a certain distance in life. When another cycle is completed, it carries us on further. As we pass through one cycle after another, we will continue to move on in God's life. If at some point our experience of the cycle stops, we also come to a stop in God's life. These are the words of one who really knew God and who knew the Word of God.

Therefore, brothers and sisters, it is in the law of life and in the intuition, that we know God. This is very practical. This knowing does not need the teaching of others at all. This is the climax of the new covenant. This is also the glory of the new covenant. Hallelujah! Here we must praise and worship Him.

A FINAL WORD

We have spoken a great deal concerning the characteristic of the new covenant. But to really know and understand it, we must have the revelation and the illumination of the Holy Spirit. We must remember that the letter kills, but the Spirit gives life (2 Cor. 3:6). The Lord said: "It is the Spirit Who gives life; the flesh profits nothing" (John 6:63). Apart from the Holy Spirit nothing can quicken man.

The new covenant is a great grace; it is very rich and most glorious. Therefore, we need to ask God to give us faith. What is faith? Hebrews 11:1 says, "Now faith is the substantiating of things hoped for, the conviction of things not seen." This is the definition of faith in the Scripture. What is the meaning of substance? In the Greek language it means a foundation, a standing, or a supporting ground. For example, if we put a book on the bookshelf, it is the bookshelf which is holding the book. Or, if we sit on a chair, it is the chair which supports us.

The word "conviction" has the sense of proving, which has the nature of a verb. Faith upholds the things we hoped for, allowing our heart to be at rest. The faith within can prove the unseen things to us, so that our heart can say "amen" to the words which God has spoken. Faith is the foundation or supporting ground which holds the things we hoped for; faith is the proof of things unseen. Second Corinthians 1:20 says: "For how many soever be the promises of God, in him is the yea: wherefore also through him is the Amen, unto the glory of God through us." Therefore, we do not look at ourselves but unto Him, Christ. His blood is the base of the new covenant. He has bequeathed to us the entire spiritual inheritance, and He is also the Executor of the testament, or will. What can be more secure than this?

God is faithful (Heb. 10:23). God's faithfulness is the guarantee of His promises, and the guarantee of His covenant (Deut. 7:9; Psa. 89:33-34). If we do not believe, we commit an offense against God's faithfulness and consider Him to be a liar. Therefore, whenever we find it difficult to believe, on the one hand, we need to condemn the unbelief as sin and ask the Lord to remove the evil heart of unbelief (Heb. 3:12); on the other hand, we need to look away unto Jesus, the Author and Perfecter of faith (Heb. 12:2). Since the Lord has created the initial faith in us (Eph. 2:8; 1 Tim. 1:14; 2 Pet. 1:1), we believe that He will also bring this faith to perfection. Oh, blessed and glorious new covenant! Let us not be too late in believing. We have repented and shed tears many times because we are so poor. We must admit that we have limited God too much and are too far short of the standards of the new covenant.

Many times, brothers and sisters, it is not that we do not seek, but that we seek in the wrong way. This is a shame. We are too much in the letter and too much dependent upon ourselves. For this reason we struggle and strive. The result is only a sigh of pain. The following hymn will help remind us not to seek further in the wrong way.

> It is not by struggling,
> But by yielding all,
> I may rest from labor,
> All my burden fall.
> It is not resolving,
> But Thyself to heed,
> I'm from sin delivered
> And from bondage freed.
>
> It is not by letter,
> But by Spirit 'tis,
> I will be approved,
> Share Thy life of bliss.
> It is not man's teaching,
> But anointing Thine,
> Which imparts Thy light and
> Fellowship divine.

It is not resolving
    Now to run the race,
But 'tis by Thy mercy
    I receive Thy grace.
It is not by knowledge,
    But by grace alone,
I can pass through suff'ring
    To Thine image grown.

Not by lofty phrases,
    But by power Thine,
I the lost can pilot
    Unto life divine.
It is not my wisdom,
    But Thy Spirit, Lord,
Which alone can fit me
    To fulfill Thy Word.

(*Hymns,* 751)

In closing, let us exercise our heart to read two passages of Scripture and so express our deep longing and our heart's desire. The first is Hebrews 13:20-21 which says: "Now the God of peace Who brought up from among the dead our Lord Jesus, the great Shepherd of the sheep, by the blood of an eternal covenant, equip you in every good work for the doing of His will, doing in us that which is well-pleasing in His sight through Jesus Christ, to Whom be the glory forever and ever, Amen." The second passage is Ephesians 3:20-21: "But to Him Who is able to do superabundantly above all that we ask or think, according to the power which operates in us, to Him be the glory in the church and in Christ Jesus unto all the generations of the age of the ages. Amen."